good
fORtUNe

starsignsstarsigns

good
fORtUNe

starsignsstarsigns

Michele Knight

MQP
MQ Publications Ltd

Published by **MQ Publications Limited**
12 The Ivories, 6–8 Northampton Street
London N1 2HY
Tel: 020 7359 2244   Fax: 020 7359 1616
email: mail@mqpublications.com

Copyright © MQ Publications Limited 2002

TEXT © **Michele Knight** 2002
DESIGN: **Balley Design**

ISBN: 1-84072-369-6

3 5 7 9 0 8 6 4 2

Printed and bound in China

Introduction

Your star sign is your outer persona—your vehicle in the world, or your ego. It influences how others perceive you. As you become older, you grow into your star sign and, if you know how, you can use it to your advantage. Have you ever wondered why you encounter certain patterns in your life? Have you been lucky in some areas of your life, and not in others? This book aims to reveal the secrets of your sign. Each sign has been given a number of extra gifts to enable it to succeed and shine. Different types of good fortune were bestowed upon each of the twelve signs, as well as unique strengths and weaknesses. Is every Scorpio a lying double-dealer? Are all Arians loudmouthed slobs? Or is there more to every sign than meets the eye?

If you can clearly see your strengths and weaknesses then you will have the power to make your life exactly what you want it to be. Instead of moaning about things not happening in your life, you can clear out the debris and harness your special magic. Your dreams are just a step away! Read on to see what makes you tick and how you can achieve your dreams faster.

ARies

March 21 – April 20

Star Profile

KEY WORDS	Spontaneity, windfalls, fame, drive, energy
RULING PLANET	Mars, god of war and passion
LUCKY AT	Making things happen, sports, comedy
AVOID	Recklessness, aggression, impetuous acts

As the first sign of the zodiac, you Arians seem to have been given a large helping of good fortune. First in line for all things, your eagerness and zest for life always give you a helping hand. You have an innate belief not only in yourself but also in miracles. You love a challenge, and your self-confidence and bravado make you fearless when chasing your dreams. Even though you balk at the idea that life is determined by fate (you have too much ego for that—you love to direct your life) you still, like the baby of the zodiac that you are, believe in magic.

The good news for Arians is that good fortune pops into your life on a regular basis. You exude just the right kind of energy to bring Lady Luck knocking on your door. Your impulsive, exuberant, and eager attitude inspires good fortune. You might be reckless, impetuous, and downright crazy at times, but when you decide to turn your life around to increase your flow of abundance, there is no measure too drastic for you to consider. This natural audacity leads to many interesting scenarios and some amazing adventures.

Impulsive or Impossible?

You see yourself as a knight in shining armor: Whether you're male or female, you have a tendency to want to save the world. You don't go about this in a practical way—you would run into a burning building to save a maiden or small children because it would raise your self-esteem. How can you harness this energy to your full advantage?

Take some time to look closely at your life and examine your reckless, impetuous nature. Has it led to some major dramas? I think so! Finding the balance and learning to think before you leap is the key to turning your fortune around. Think through the consequences of what you are about to do. Lady Luck can't help you unless you help yourself. Think about what might happen if you chuck that glass of wine at your boss because he was rude!

However, you tend to land on your feet no matter what stunts you pull. The gods always seem to be smiling down on you—they must admire your gall! To harness this natural luck, focus on what you are good at. Because you are such a passionate creature, good luck only turns away from you when you conform or are doing something you detest. You were born to follow your dreams and to cut a swath through the masses with your originality.

Aries Tip

Although the symbol for you
Arians is the ram, try not to headbutt your way to good fortune!
Even with all your charm and charisma, appearing to be a bully can
hold you back. You tend to be one step ahead of everyone else,
so you should learn tolerance and patience, which is
exactly what you expect from others. Using your
allure, rather than just going straight in with
your horns, will increase abundance in
your life. In fact, you hate being the
bad guy, so show off that gorgeous
openness and encourage other people
with love rather than commands.

LUCKY COLORS

Red is a great color for you, but your lucky color is purple. The mixture of blue and red that is in purple will balance you: Red for your fiery, passionate nature, and for your ruling planet Mars, and blue to calm you so you don't explode with enthusiasm or anger! Wear something purple if you're in a situation where you need to remain calm, yet energized. Paint a room lilac or lavender for complete relaxation. This room will feel nurturing and protective, increasing your sense of well-being and relaxation. However, if you do wear red you will look fabulous!

Having one red room in the house will increase your energy and passion for life. A great room to paint red is the bathroom. Fill it with gold-framed paintings or accessories—this will balance your base passion with spiritual gold, and you will find that when you have a bath you recharge your energy. Try burning some gold candles and **throw in some carnelian crystals to make you feel charged up and refreshed.** (However, if you find that you feel irritated or bad-tempered, remove the crystals immediately—you are passionate enough already!) **This is a great thing to do with your partner** and will certainly put you in the mood for love.

Be True to You

You can do anything you put your mind to. You were born to be different, and failure is not in your vocabulary. For example, Leonardo da Vinci was an Aries. His passion and originality created some of the most incredible art the world has known. Charlie Chaplin strove to create comedy that was unlike anyone else's. You Arians are originators. The fire of success is inside you; you hunger for it, you need it, and whatever that elusive word "success" means to you, you can and will achieve it.

One thing that can set you back is your tendency to start things and not finish them. Your passion for a project or your belief in a dream starts off like a hurricane and ends up a drizzle. Your tolerance for boredom is very low; you need to build on your stamina to increase your chances of success. If you don't give up, you will definitely succeed.

Here's a great tip for you Arians: As soon as you find yourself grumbling about work or find your mind wandering, rekindle your passion for what you are doing by visualizing the successful outcome and reminding yourself why you are doing it in the first place. Remember your initial desire and zeal and reawaken it.

Increase your luck by choosing a profession that you can excel in, and which has a certain amount of adventure and changeability. You hate routine, and a nine-to-five existence puts a real strain on you. You are a natural fighter and can succeed in any job that you find personally challenging. Arians have traditionally been cast in the role of soldiers, sportsmen and -women, and firefighters—all jobs that require courage and a certain amount of gall!

Whether you are male or female, you will have an added edge when going for a job interview, because interviews require courage. If you were auditioning for *Survivor* and were told that you would be stranded on a desert island with six thousand poisonous reptiles, you wouldn't bat an eyelid. Be bold: Whether you're interested in becoming a teacher or traveling the world in search of the long-lost city of Atlantis, go for it! Good fortune will follow.

Give Fortune a Helping Hand

You typically hinder yourself by not planning—this is definitely an area in which you lack practical skills. You think you can take that trip to the Arctic with only your jeans and a pair of boots, but that charming naïveté can ruin your chances of success . . . and also leave you with frostbite and no toes! Good fortune can't strike if you aren't prepared, so give luck a helping hand by planning. Get into the habit of making lists of things you may need to take if you are going shopping, planning an adventure, or going to a job interview. This simple technique can increase your success rate and enable your dreams to become reality. Don't believe me? Try it!

You tend to ram your way forward, ignoring all obstacles, and keep going against all odds. Although this is admirable and worthy, sometimes the best way to invite good fortune can be to surrender. Realize that surrendering to a higher power is not defeat but an act of trust! Trust that you are meant to get there because you are worth it. Trust that life has magic in it, especially for you! Life will lead you in the right direction in the subtlest of ways and surprise you with all sorts of lucky breaks. Hammering away at your goal is fine, but when you have done the hard work it can be more effective to stand back and allow life to bring you your reward.

LUCKY GEMSTONES

Diamonds are both a girl's best friend and the power stones of all Arians. A diamond is very similar to you: sparkling, strong, and practically indestructible. If you can afford this precious jewel, wear it as a talisman to attract the riches you deserve. Give it to a loved one as an Aries love token and it will help protect your relationship.

The **garnet** is your passion stone. This jewel pulses with sensuality and is great if you feel run-down or lacking in passion. Garnets help you exude sexuality and can make you a winner in love.

Amethyst is a balancing stone and increases your wisdom. To make an important decision, sit down for a few minutes holding your amethyst in your left hand (your left hand receives energy and your right hand gives energy). Visualize the purple energy flowing around your body, touching your intuition and inner wisdom.

LUCKY *numbers*

Aries, your lucky numbers are one, nine, eight, and eleven. You can be particularly lucky at games with dice, but, as with all things, you tend not to know when to stop. Gambling is therefore a pursuit that you should try to avoid. The adrenalin rush of gambling can be totally addictive for you, and is not conducive to your good fortune!

If you want to find your own personal lucky number, get some dice, throw them twenty times, and jot down which numbers come up. Repeat this process for three days and you will be amazed at the results.

Aries Tip

Ylang-ylang is your oil. It keeps you balanced and in touch with your more gentle side. Ylang-ylang is thought to be an antidepressant, so it is great to use if you lose your belief or trust in the universe. This deep, sensual smell is also said to be an aphrodisiac, and so is great to put in an oil burner if you have a date. Remember: What you believe, you create. Your positive attitude is half your power.

Lucky Aries

There are so many of you lucky Arians; you have the gift of capturing each and every opportunity and going for it with your childlike belief.

Warren Beatty, for example, was very lucky with the ladies. You Arians love the hunt and adore flirting and chasing. Beatty excelled in this Arian sport. Though he allegedly bedded such babes as Madonna and Julie Christie, he eventually settled down—when he was ready—with Annette Bening and had three children. Because you are a fire sign, you will love with all the fire you have in you when you make a commitment. But don't offer it too quickly! Bite that impulsive tongue of yours. Warren was smart and avoided committing too soon. He is successful, had some mind-blowing lovers, and enjoyed his freedom until he was ready. This tale is perfect for you Arians: Don't make a commitment until you are ready. Good fortune follows when you truly follow your heart, so don't try to please other people for the sake of it. Be sensitive and honest, but never, ever make rash decisions in love. You're exactly the type to run off to Las Vegas and get married in the Elvis chapel of love, but remember: Don't let your romantic spontaneity include commitment unless you are absolutely certain!

Lucky man
Warren Beatty

On the Other Hand . . .

Harry Houdini gave the world a run for his money! He started off stricken by poverty, but made it to the top in true Arian style. His passion for his work and his Arian habit of being totally fearless made certain that he never knew when to quit. It is said that he ended up dying because of his ramlike bravado. A student punched him in the stomach (a typical Arian party trick is to show off your strength!), and for once he wasn't prepared. The punch ruptured his appendix, and this caused a major illness. However, he still viewed himself as indestructible and carried on with his work when he should have been in bed. Learn from Harry's typically Arian mistake: Take time to stop and enjoy your good fortune when you make it. Nonstop pushing can lead to exhaustion and bad health.

Vincent van Gogh had the creative ability that is latent in all Arians. He painted in the vibrant colors that Arians love and was truly unique. He was allegedly driven mad as a result of being misunderstood and his talent being unappreciated (he never sold a painting during his life). In a fit of anger he cut off his ear. This intense anger can be just under the surface of the Arian personality. To keep your good fortune when you find it, it is essential never to lose your belief in yourself.

Harness the Fire

Harnessing your fantastic drive is the key to your success. Be very focused about what you want to achieve, and **visualize it clearly in your mind**—as if it has already happened. What does it feel like now that you have achieved your dream? What do your clothes and your surroundings look and smell like? How have you changed now that you **have fulfilled all your ambitions? Visualization is a powerful tool for you**. High achievers are considered to have exceptional skill at visualizing scenarios. Could this be the secret of their success?

tAURUS

April 21 – May 21

STAR PROFILE

KEY WORDS	Determination, security, sensuality, cooking
RULING PLANET	Venus, goddess of love
LUCKY AT	Homemaking, designing, self-employment, inheritances
AVOID	Laziness, self-indulgence, greed, weight gain

All star signs have special gifts and skills that, if followed, will lead them to good fortune and their ultimate goals. The good fortune that was bestowed upon you Taureans is your ability to stubbornly head toward your desires. You also possess loyalty and sensuality. These traits impress others and you are often chosen above competitors, particularly in career scenarios.

So what can stop you from achieving all that you desire? Where does Lady Luck leave you standing in the rain? You have a fear of the new. You love routine and security and when it is time to take a risk you sometimes hem and haw until the opportunity has passed. It can take you years to move or to change your career. To help your own good fortune you need to get in touch with your intuition—and not always rely on the familiar—to give you what you need. Always remember that you are a bull—a powerful creature that is utterly unstoppable. Unless you meet a bullfighter with a cape, nothing can bring you down except fear.

Take a Walk on the Wild Side

How can you best use your potential? How can you attract the attention of the gods to bring you all that you dream of? You have to decide exactly what it is that you want! It is impossible to bring about something that doesn't exist in your head.

Think about your home or your lover—are these areas that you'd want to change or improve? Because you can be so at home with the familiar, you can be quite content with your bunny slippers and run-down shack. But remember: Familiarity breeds contempt for glistening good fortune. Take a look at your life now. Are you happy where you live? Are you happy with your lover? What are your desires for the future? You have to dream it to have it. I know it takes time, but start to dream it! Relax: All of this is in your hands. You can set the pace, but remember that you can achieve anything when you put your mind to it. Go inside and decide how you want good fortune to strike!

If you fall in love with an idea, such as acting or painting, your Taurean abilities will blossom and you would probably become the best there is. You are persistent and if you love what you're doing you want to do it all the time. Because you are compulsive you can use this to your advantage to attract good fortune!

LUCKY GEMSTONES

Emeralds are your birthstone and they are a fabulous choice. They are thought to be excellent for protection in love and for attracting money. This magical gem seems to know no bounds in what it can attract. Emeralds resonate to the heart's *chakra*, or center of energy. Hold the emerald against your heart to heal the past and open you to new love.

Moss agate, another lucky gemstone for you, is a gorgeous crystal that is cheap, cheerful, and beautiful. It looks like clear quartz with green moss inside. Native Americans treasure this stone, and it is great for grounding you and balancing your energy so that you feel better about yourself.

LUCKY COLORS

Your colors are baby blue and pink—probably because these were the first colors you saw as an infant and, as we know, you are a creature of habit! Blue is the color of communication. It can help you, as you often have trouble with your throat. Visualizing light blue in and around your throat may help you to communicate, and can even soothe a sore throat. Another good color for you is green. Taureans are wonderful gardeners and have naturally green thumbs. Gardening is a great stress reliever, so go plant and watch it grow. Green also has a balancing effect on the eyes and can help to alleviate headaches and eyestrain. Painting a bedroom green will create a soothing space for you to relax and, as green is the color of the heart center, you will feel at peace with your partner in this room. To create a bond between you and your partner or to feel safe, snuggle up on the sofa, with a green rug below. Green can also helps to combat that typically Taurean jealous streak!

Learn to Let Go

One thing you need to watch out for is your possessive attitude. People notice this and it can make them get a little worried. You may have high standards when it comes to loyalty, but make sure that you are not hindering your own and others' success by coveting other people's things. To want to possess something (or someone) indicates that you do not believe in the power of the universe to always provide you with what you need. You sometimes cling so tightly to prized objects or people that you can end up losing out in the long run. Get rid of this kind of mentality and you will be able to see the infinite power of your life: the ability to naturally manifest what you desire.

You also have fabulous potential for making—and, more important, keeping—money! You are incredibly good with finances and, because you adore the good things in life, you are careful with it in just the right way. Like a squirrel, you almost always have a secret store stashed away in the bank for emergencies. This hoarding instinct helps you immensely, particularly as you get older and wealthier.

One quality you have that enhances as well as negates your luck is your stubbornness. Learn to use this skill like a ninja warrior.

Transform your stubbornness into an art form so that it works for you. It's no good being pigheaded in an emotional situation, for instance, because this reduces communication and hinders the relationship. If your partner gives in to your stubbornness, you have won a battle with underhanded tactics. So keep your natural stubbornness out of your personal relationships, but use it to achieve your goals in other areas of your life, like getting into shape or sticking to a meditation routine.

The good news is that you are a shockingly good lover, with amazing stamina, and people tend to forgive you when they feel the brush of your fingertips on their bare skin. Don't let this charming streak let you become too demanding; you can get away with murder, but don't you want to be the best bull you can be?

Your stamina can help you turn your life around, so build yourself up gradually with a more positive outlook. Set yourself small goals, like that of apologizing freely when you feel you may have been too harsh, and breaking your routines when they become too rigid. You have limitless choices and each new reality that you create will become as comfortable to you as your favorite slippers. When you reach your goal you are in a better position than most other star signs to stay there, so banish any thoughts of failure and get started right this second.

Taurus Tip

Practice the art of flexibility. If
you were more flexible you would be almost perfect and life would
be a dream. In every important situation allow yourself to bend a
little and to put yourself in others' shoes. Avoid having a fixed
view on anything. Let each problem in life be seen as a
gift that brings you to your next level of
awareness. Instead of resisting and pushing,
try different forms of communicating
and make a concerted effort to go
with the flow. You will notice instant
rewards if you acquire flexibility.

LUCKY *numbers*

Lucky numbers for Taureans are six, four, twelve, and twenty-two. However, you tend to get so attached to things that you may well have your own special lucky numbers! Positive belief creates good fortune, so stick to these numbers if you feel that they are lucky. You are not much of a gambler (although you occasionally buy a lottery ticket) because you only like a sure thing. If you are bitten by the gambling bug, however, it usually becomes a destructive habit. Habits— even bad ones—make you feel secure. Once you develop a taste for something, it is virtually impossible to get you unhooked unless you use your stubbornness to get you out of it.

Lucky Taurus

You only have to look at Cher and Barbra Streisand to see that if a Taurus loves something, they remain fantastic at it forever. Both these women have more than survived in the music business and have that Taurean gift of staying on top. Years may come and go, but these two carry on working, getting better and better. Cher's last album was her most successful, and Barbra's concerts are packed to the rafters no matter what the price of the ticket. You go, girls!

James Brown can also be included in this group of Taureans who are familiar with glory. William Shakespeare (another Taurus) adored writing, and is arguably the best-known writer in the universe! If you Taureans like a position you stay there, and nothing can topple you. Because you inspire loyalty, other people in the business will remember you, respect you, and help keep you at the top. You really enjoy networking and love to mix with others who are at your level. This is a great asset, but don't turn into a snob!

Let these supremely well-known Taurean role models be an inspiration for your unquestionable potential.

Lucky Taurus Cher still at the top of her profession ☞

On the Other Hand . . .

The unsavory Adolf Hitler was, in fact, a Taurus (some astrologers mistakenly think he was an Aries). Hitler had lots of planets in Taurus and is a terrible example of a Taurean megalomaniac. Many despots have been Taureans, clinging onto their views no matter how destructive they are. This need to be in control can bring about the downfall of a Taurus and, indeed, those who surround them. Hitler is, of course, a terrible caricature of Taurean bad points, but his stubbornness and his belief that he was always right are Taurean traits—no matter how hard you'd like to deny it. The lesson to be learned is this: Do not be too dogmatic. Stretch your views and accept all people as equal. Do not be a control freak, under any circumstances.

Harness the Earth

One of your greatest skills is your tenacity. If you believe in something you will naturally head toward it and ignore anything that gets in the way. You have the ability to succeed with good, old-fashioned hard work and you know it. If you have a dream in mind, write down a detailed plan of what it will look like when it is completed. Get a large piece of paper and draw a treasure map. Plot your journey toward your "treasure" (the treasure being the outcome you desire). Check off the places you pass as you do the things that lead you to your goal. Visual incentives like this allow you to remain focused.

gemiNi

May 22 – June 21

StAR pROFile

KEY WORDS	Flexibility, deftness, ideas, writing, ruling
RULING PLANET	Mercury, god of communication
LUCKY AT	Being eloquent, creating, computers, public relations
AVOID	Fickleness, being superficial, lying, being unfaithful

Do you Geminis believe in all this good fortune nonsense? Well, yes and no! You see both sides of every story and like to understand all concepts. Your rational mind has a very Darwinian approach to life: scientific, reasoned, and unusually practical. Yet deep within your psyche you have an intuition that comes from your sharp mind. You are like a lightning bolt, and can change your mind and your life path from one millisecond to the next.

Your good fortune is connected to your ability to change your life at will—when you decide to do something, you have the willpower to make it happen and are not afraid of change. Few star signs are gifted with this love of intellectual challenge and change.

When you were a child, you were probably dressing like a disco diva one minute and like a grungy punk rocker the next. You like to experience and taste all that life has to offer.

The Social Animal

You are an excellent mover and shaker, and public relations is a good field for you. You love chitchat and are a charming, charismatic individual. People like to have you around because you are so witty and engaging. Take full advantage of this by taking the time to build up a good contact base, rather than just flitting from party to party. Good fortune may strike, and the perfect contact to complete the deal will already be in your Rolodex from that tedious lunch you attended last year. Good fortune is there for you everywhere because of your gift for communication.

You may find that you are skilled at interpreting trends in the music industry, and of sensing when something new is on the horizon. Using this skill can bring untold rewards. Developing your quickness and intellectual ability will give you an edge. The written word holds a fascination for you, and many well-known writers— from the poet Thomas Hardy to Ian Fleming of James Bond fame— have been Geminis. Harness this interest and turn it from a hobby into a moneymaker. Your ruling planet is Mercury, the planet of communication, so all areas of communication resonate well with you. You may have amazing skills when it comes to computers or telephones. Check it out and build up those skills.

LUCKY GEMSTONES

Agates are very lucky gems indeed, and you automatically resonate with them. There are many types of agate, from blue lace agate (which promotes truth and to help verbal expression) to polka-dot agate (which creates cheerfulness and a feeling of well-being). In Roman times, agates were carried for luck. Today, they are considered versatile and strong talismans. Although not officially your stone, **rose quartz** opens up the heart chakra and can get you in touch with your emotions. It helps heal broken hearts, and as the traditional love stone can possibly even draw love to you. **Amber** is often called a gem even though it is really petrified sap. This gem has a grounding effect on you and will help keep your feet on the ground. It also helps mop up negative energy to keep you clear-headed.

With your quick wit and sharp senses, you are often in the right place at the right time when opportunity or luck shows itself. You can spot a good prospect at twenty paces. However, you are also liable to sabotage yourself because of your idealistic view that life is full of different opportunities: When you get bored you tend to rocket off to the next exciting destination. All this unpredictable stuff is great, but it can lead you down dead-end roads. And while it's true that many opportunities exist in life, seeing one of your projects all the way through to completion can bring great benefits to you. Building sound foundations and making sure you plan ahead will help you achieve what you desire.

You are an explorer of the human mind, so you should take a look at your thought patterns. How do you relate to yourself in your own head? Are you a kind person? Do you have a healthy, positive inner dialogue, or do you give yourself a hard time? Taking the time and energy to heal your inner voice will boost your energy levels and will to succeed.

lucky *numbers*

Lucky numbers for Geminis are three, six, thirty-three, and fifteen. Because you are an excellent mathematician and good with numbers in general, numbers resonate with you. You have luck when guessing numbers or instinctively figuring out which numbers will come up in a card game. You like to boast about your magnificent memory, and it's true that your mind can capture numbers probably better than any other sign except Aquarius.

LUCKY COlORS

Yellow is the color of the solar plexus *chakra*: a ball of energy that represents your self-esteem and ego. As Geminis relate strongly to yellow, this is a color that you should work with. **Yellow is also the color of intellect and mental activity**. If you feel that you have too much brain energy and thoughts are circulating wildly inside your head, **do not decorate your room in yellow because it will activate your mind even more**.

Only you lucky Geminis could have the rainbow as your colors. Perhaps this is because you can never make up your mind and enjoy change. The rainbow is an important symbol for you, and reminds you that you will find your pot of gold! Wondrous, eclectic creature that you are, you would benefit by having a study or creative room decorated in the colors of the rainbow: Paint the walls different colors in blocks, squares, or stripes. Find pieces of artwork that inspire you, or experiment and make your own art. You need a space to go wild in if you live in a small apartment, so choose a corner where you can experience this rainbow color rush, or have a trunk with paints and rugs, oils, diaries, photos, and music where you can open up and excite your senses whenever you are stressed out.

Are You a Tease?

Flirty Geminis know how to entertain and delight. Cupid often sits on your shoulder and takes random potshots at passersby, just for fun. As a result, you find that emotions and situations sweep through you like a storm. One minute you have met the man or woman of your dreams, and the next, that dream has turned stale. You lose interest quickly, which can leave many ranting ex-partners behind ready to annihilate your reputation. Good fortune gave you the gift of being a love magnet: You are aided by your association with the winged messenger, Mercury.

People listen when you talk. Although your sharp mind allows you to hijack conversations that are halfway through, you must learn to listen and be quiet when necessary. You can be a terrible gossip if you're bored, but this does not suit you because you're a decent individual who is not judgmental. You are a creature of words, so if you use these tools carefully, and not for spite, you will cause people to speak only good things of you. It's simple, really, but creates good karma all round! You're very good at communicating effectively with the world. Study the way you talk and pay attention to what you talk about, and this will reveal what you feel that you have achieved in your life. You may be surprised!

Gemini Tip

Don't analyze your emotions, but rather build
up an awareness of your feelings. If you feel emotionally
stuck, go and see a sad movie or put on some soul-
stirring music to shift into your feeling side.
With the right balance between thought
and heart you will travel through
your life on a much clearer
path. Don't be overanalytical or
chase your thoughts in circles.
Value your rich, emotional self as
much as your vast intellect.

Lucky Gemini

Beautiful Oscar winner Halle Berry is a feisty Gemini. She's overcome huge odds to become one of America's top actors. Raised in the American Midwest, her mother, a psychiatric nurse, brought her up. Her father is alleged to have been abusive and frequently absent from the family home. She was taunted and bullied through high school, and when she was voted prom queen, had to share the title with a white student to suppress the uproar. She experienced many problems in relationships, and one boyfriend beat her so severely that she is still 80 percent deaf in one ear.

Did all this destroy Halle? No! Her Gemini star was set to rise, and through her gutsy determination she set the world on fire with such films as Spike Lee's *Jungle Fever*. After receiving the Best Actress Oscar in 2002, there will be no stopping her. You Geminis have the rare ability of always trying something new, of taking on life from many different perspectives, until you finally find the right road. Never give in and your brilliance will become apparent regardless of what anyone thinks.

The inspirational Josephine Baker—actress, singer, and dancer—had an amazing life and created her own luck. This

Gemini achieved fame and had remarkable adventures. Her talent, beauty, and love of humanity made her stand out. She became involved in the French Resistance during World War II and worked as an intelligence officer. As a Gemini she was no doubt a natural chameleon, and was a very successful spy.

Josephine Baker communicated her mercurial charisma through music and movement, bringing her many admirers. She posed for the artist Alexander Calder, and adopted twelve children of different nationalities, which she called her "rainbow tribe." She was active in living her life in support of other African Americans, using her ability to communicate effectively to fight for justice.

Academy Award winner and Gemini Halle Berry

On the Other Hand . . .

Isadora Duncan was a typical Gemini. She was years ahead of her time: a dancer in the Roaring Twenties whose vision created modern dance. This woman took dance out of the Victorian era and birthed it as a creative and individual expression. Perhaps only a Gemini could have done this. Unconventional, she viewed marriage as a prison and rebelliously had two children with two different lovers. Her mercurial love of freedom and adventure led her to set up unique dance schools all over Europe and America.

Her Gemini originality led her to live a dazzling life full of love, but sadly also of tragedy. At the peak of her fame her two children died in a freak car accident that was a terrible foreboding of how she herself would die. Carrying on her work and recognized as the genius she was, Isadora went on to adopt six children, whom she also taught to dance.

Isadora loved to wear long, flowing silk scarves, and as she was being driven through the streets of Paris her scarf got tangled in the back wheel of her car, strangling her. Gone but not forgotten, her unique interpretation of movement lives on in contemporary dance troupes: the interpretation of free expression.

Harness the Air

You are tempted to drift off on tangents. You were blessed with an abundance of ideas and sparks of genius, yet you flit in your mind from concept to concept and are often unable to decide which ideas you should develop. Jot down all your ideas, but make sure that you plan and follow them up. You could have been a genius ten times over and made an impressive fortune with your innovations. The only thing stopping you is your inability to follow through. Always keep a notebook or tape recorder nearby to capture the precious gems that come to you. Your mind is your fortune.

CANCER

June 22 – July 22

STAR PROFILE

KEY WORDS	Loving, mothering, nurturing, caring
RULING PLANET	The Moon, goddess of emotion and fertility
LUCKY AT	Teaching, partnership, counseling, cookery
AVOID	Insecurity, manipulation, avoidance, suppressed anger

What did the fates give to Cancer that you can benefit from? You are a great nurturer and are very good with people, children, and in the home. You may not see these qualities as great gifts, but they are, and don't forget it. However, Cancer often lacks confidence, particularly early on in life, but to take full advantage of your natural good fortune, you cannot give in to your insecurities. If you're not open to good fortune, how can it find you?

You are supremely talented and deeply connected to your own intuition. There are many fields that you can excel in once you understand that you can make your fortune doing what you enjoy and what comes naturally to you!

Love Yourself as You Love Others

You have the terrible habit of putting yourself down, and this can stop your flow of creativity and life energy. You may get stuck in a dead-end job or relationship and feel powerless, fearing change, but you've just got to climb out from behind that shell and steer your life in a more enjoyable direction. You're a survivor, and if you focus and act on what you want, you will get it.

Let's take a look at what you're good at and what you adore. The fates decree that you should be exceptionally good in all matters related to the home. With a bit of imaginative thinking you can turn this into a thriving business in interior design. You have a natural flair for what looks fabulous and, more important, cozy and homely. You can make the latest design trends attractive and accessible because you bring warmth to all you touch. You have the ability to put everyone at ease when they step into your home, and others would love to be able to have that gift.

You are also great with people and kids and would excel as a teacher or a counselor. You have a deep intuitive ability, which helps you get to the core of others' problems. More important, you actually care about these problems. Instead of doing this in your spare time and being the ear that everyone turns to, take

LUCKY GEMSTONES

The **moonstone** is your stone and is fabulous for
you. It will help you balance yourself to be able to go with
the flow. Moonstones are also great for fertility (they symbolize
the egg), so if you want to get pregnant, great. If not, watch out!
Pearls are unlucky for some, but very lucky for you. They
draw you in and make you feel safe and secure.
It seems that you are more confident when
wearing pearls, and as a classic accessory
they will never go out of fashion. If you
are a man, get some cufflinks or a
tie tack with a pearl
on it, or carry one in
your wallet to
increase your
finances.

some classes and get paid for doing what you adore. Cancers make great teachers because students feel at ease in their presence and want to work! If they are in the right employment, Cancers love their jobs, which is part of the key to their success.

Another skill that the gods bequeathed to you is your natural flair for cooking. Taureans may be the best gardeners, but you Cancers are the best cooks. You love to eat and you love to feed people. Open a restaurant or invent the next must-have cookie recipe. Turn that great salad dressing into an international business! You put your love into your cooking and that makes it taste unique. You are blessed with an abundance of good fortune and you may not have even known it until now. One key to turning your fortune around is forgetting yesterday or last year and living in the moment. Right now you can do anything. If you decide that your life will transform in this very second, you're halfway there.

LUCKY *numbers*

Lucky numbers for Cancer are three, six, thirty-three, and fifteen. Because you are an excellent mathematician and good with numbers in general, numbers resonate with you. You have luck when guessing numbers or instinctively figuring out which numbers will come up in a card game. You like to boast about your magnificent memory, and it's true that your mind can capture numbers probably better than any other sign except Aquarius.

LUCKY COLORS

Soft, muted colors, such as cream and white, are good for you because they resemble your ruler, the moon. All colors associated with water, such as sea blue, green, and silver, also resonate with you. When you are surrounded by these colors, it feels like a weight has been lifted from your shoulders, and to have your bedroom in clean whites and creams, with white linen sheets, creates feelings of sensuality and security. You love to wear silver jewelry and would benefit from any green, blue, or white stones. You look fabulous in white linen or cotton, which gives you a sense of confidence. If you feel vulnerable or exposed, color-visualization can help you protect your energy: Shut your eyes and imagine a silver light all around your body. This bubble will protect your aura. As you have a habit of picking up others' emotions, imagining this bright, silver light stops you from merging with others so much and becoming drained.

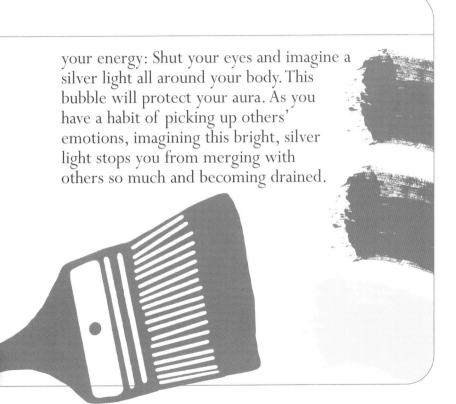

Let It Go

As a crab you are blessed in many ways. You were given that tough shell to shield your sensitive center and to help you survive the rough and tumble of life. It doesn't always feel like good fortune to you that you are more sensitive than most, but trust me: That shell is there for a reason, and when you learn to combine your emotions and fully use your protection you will be better equipped than most to turn your life around. You just have to go for it. Perhaps you need to discuss your dreams with someone practical who can help you. Try chatting with a Leo friend about how to unearth all that magic.

Don't let your gift of sensitivity become a curse. Take a page out of an Arian's book and learn to bounce back and put the past behind you. See the positive in all situations and trust that all failures happen because there is something even more spectacular out there for you.

Something that can block you is your attachment to the past. You can hurt for years over situations that have long passed. Okay: So Jeffrey stood you up at the prom, you were humiliated, and you still blush at the thought of that night. In fact, you still think about that night on a regular basis. Stop it! It was a blessing in disguise!

Cancer Tip

You are particularly
affected by the cycles of the Moon. You have the ability to
tune yourself into the rhythm of the Moon and increase your energy,
and possibly your abundance. Get a calendar, figure out which
cycle the Moon is in, and observe your moods and
energy levels during an entire month's cycle. When
do you feel better? At the new Moon or full
Moon? The full Moon is an energizer
and is great if you are building up a
project, while the new Moon is good
for releasing and starting new projects
as well as asking for a wish
to be granted.

Lucky Cancer

Sylvester Stallone was born in a charity hospital. His father was a hairdresser and his mother was a dancer. He was apparently a shy child with typical Cancer sensitivity. He once had a job cleaning out lions' cages. Determined to be an actor, he wrote out the script for the film *Rocky* by hand and refused to sell it unless he was given the lead role. The rest, as they say, is history. Sylvester was very close to his mother. Most Cancers have either excellent or terrible relationships with their mothers. In Sylvester's case, his mother was a savvy psychic who predicted his success!

Multi-Oscar winner (he won Oscars three years in a row!) Tom Hanks is a typical Cancer. Unlike other famous actors, he adores his family and worships his wife Rita, whom he married in 1988. He has four children and loves nothing better than spending time with them. He has achieved the ultimate Cancer good fortune: He has a loving, successful family life and the job of his dreams—in front of and behind the camera.

Lucky Cancer actor Sylvester Stallone ☛

On the Other Hand . . .

Mickey Rourke got into acting after a series of jobs, including training attack dogs and laying floors. He rose to success with his stunning performances in the controversial *9 ½ Weeks* and in *Angel Heart*. No doubt people were drawn to his good looks and intense emotions. As a Cancer man he may have found this sudden rise to fame difficult. Cancers tend to be a little insecure and feel unworthy, particularly if they have had a hard life (like Mickey). Possibly it was this insecurity and lack of self-worth that led him into professional boxing. He never succeeded in that pursuit, but did mess up one of his biggest assets—his famous face. One of the sexiest men of the 1980s, he blew it all with his bravado. The lesson here for other Cancers is this: Don't let insecurity make you throw it all away. You are talented. Value your achievements!

Harness the Water

Water has a particularly soothing effect on you. Being near the ocean or even a stream instantly boosts your energy levels and makes you feel as if you have come home. If you are ever stressed out or indecisive, go and sit by some flowing water. Visualize your negativity or blocks being washed away. Take up whitewater rafting, go diving, skinny-dipping, or just plain paddling. Anything that involves playing in water gives you a buzz and is certain to make you feel as good as new. Try it!

leo

July 23 – August 22

STAR PROFILE

KEY WORDS	Loyal, regal, proud, charismatic
RULING PLANET	The Sun, god of personality
LUCKY AT	Performing, the arts, achieving goals, high ideals
AVOID	Arrogance, pomposity, extravagance

Leo, you are one of the few star signs who knows that you have been blessed. You have an innate confidence that allows you to believe in yourself. That gift has taken you this far in life, and can take you wherever you need to go.

You are endowed with the knowledge that you are special and deserve good fortune. This knowledge, as arrogant as it seems, is what makes you lucky: If you believe that you deserve something, you will proceed down all the right paths until you've found your success. When you popped out of the womb you sensed that you were here for a reason: Never take that confidence and charisma for granted. You were placed on this earth to be seen and admired.

Hang on, though—don't let this go to your head! There is a fine line between confidence and arrogance, and this is something you need to be very sure of. If you allow your confidence to be seen as arrogance, you will stumble rather than glide through life. Get the balance right and there will be no dream out of reach.

Obviously you are human and suffer from the same insecurities as the rest of us, but unlike Cancer—who may feel unworthy of success and acclaim—your lesson is to not chase it too hard. You also need to learn more compassion and sensitivity, so that when you do become a famous millionaire you are not obnoxious with it!

Lively Leos

If you want to make the most of your qualities, being a performer is an excellent career choice—from acting to concert pianist. You have the right vibes to be the next Jennifer Lopez or Ben Affleck (your Leo compatriots). If you're interested, take an acting class or piano lessons. You have a greater chance than most of succeeding in whatever fuels your passion in life.

People may think that you like to be the center of attention, and often envy the way you light up a room. This is an innate quality and beyond your control. However, being aware of other's sensitivities and insecurities will help you to avoid jealous rivals, especially in your career. Take the time to boost your colleagues' egos and be generous with your praise.

Napoleon was a typical Leo and at only five feet, four inches tall, he was the most feared man of his time. His height and looks

LUCKY GEMSTONES

Tiger-eye will not only energize you, but it is also a protection stone. It makes an excellent lucky charm for you, either worn as jewelry or just carried in your pocket. **Carnelian** reinforces your desire and gives you stamina and renewed vigor. Don't use it too much if you suffer from bad temper, as it can enhance all your emotions. **Gold** loves you and you love gold! This is a general feel-good metal for you and gives you a sense of security.

did not deter lovers; he had, arguably, the most passionate love affairs ever recorded. He was, however, also a despot! Watch out for this quality in you, because it will ultimately hold you back in life—imagine what Napoleon could have achieved with all that charisma if he had been a nice guy! If you feel that you were not graced with the good looks that your character deserves, don't become bitter and manipulative. Just know that beauty is not skin deep, and that you will be loved, and even idolized, for being your wonderful self. You have a beautiful energy that was bestowed upon you and this is your good fortune.

Arrogance is one of the few things that can make you tumble from your rightful position in life. Others see you as amazing, but if you begin to act as if you are superior, you will quite rightly be taken down a peg or two. Be aware that your ruler is the Sun and you therefore radiate self-assurance. You are one of the luckiest signs there is, and many people could never hope to have what you have.

LUCKY *numbers*

Lucky Leos should stick to five, eleven, twenty-three, fourteen, and one. All of those numbers are great for you, but one is the number of the Sun and can be particularly useful for you. It symbolizes individuality and leadership, and you are a big fan of both of those qualities.

A special magic is imparted by the number eleven, because it is a master number. A house or office with the number eleven could be especially beneficial for you, as you will be able to develop your life path and possibly achieve your life purpose there as well.

LUCKY COlORS

Yellow and orange are your colors. Yellow is the
color of the solar plexus *chakra*, which pertains to
the ego or self. When blocked, it is the center
of fear and insecurity. You are one
of the most fearless star
signs, and have a well-defined
sense of your own worth. If you
do have problems with your self-esteem,
surround yourself with yellow to boost
your self-confidence. Yellow is also the
color of the intellect and to have a study or
living room in this color encourages you to
think and communicate, but avoid having your
bedroom this color or you could find yourself
suffering from insomnia. Orange represents
sexuality and creativity. You are passionate, and

orange gives you a buzz and makes you feel uplifted and energized. Paint any room in your home orange and you will feel the zing it gives you. This color just loves you so why not embrace it! Orange flowers on the diningroom table or in your bedroom reignite your passion for life. Terracotta walls and rich fabrics with plenty of gold and maroon feel great. If you have a fireplace, make sure it becomes a center-piece for your home and light it in winter, burning pinecones for protection and well-being.

Sharing the Love

You can be incredibly lovable with a magnanimous disposition, bestowing gifts on those you love. You're always the first to put your hand in your pocket to go to the bar. This combination of looks and generosity can inspire lesser mortals to turn green with envy and, although this can lead to nasty sniping, don't take it personally: In a way, it's a twisted compliment.

Like the sunflower, a Leo symbol, you are larger than life and twice as bold. Leos were handed out double helpings of luck, but with the unwritten condition that you should always play fair. Look at your dreams and motivations and how you are attempting to succeed. Are you being selfish? Arrogant? Underhanded? Be the best that you can be and life will reward you.

You are fabulous, talented, and charismatic, so what's holding you back? Believe in yourself, because the rest of us can't help but believe in you! You've got what it takes and are lucky in all areas. The only thing that can really defeat you is yourself, so pay attention to the way you operate. If anyone else does knock you down, you always come back stronger than before and have the last laugh. It's just natural for you to be on top of the heap. You are here to make your mark on the world one way or the other!

Leo Tip

You have two major
character weaknesses: your pride and your vanity. If
someone tells you how fabulous, gorgeous, and brilliant you are, it's as
if the sun is shining on your face and you will tend to allow your
judgment to become clouded. Concentrate on the main
issue and don't become so easily distracted!
Unfortunately, your love of flattery is a well-
known secret and may be used by
unscrupulous people to manipulate
you. Wake up and smell the coffee!
Trust your instincts, and if something
smells fishy there's probably something
wet and slimy nearby!

Lucky Leo

Mick Jagger is a perfect example of a Leo man. He is not conventionally attractive—a bit scrawny with a face like a wet dishcloth—fairly short, and has an unusual dance technique. Yet none of this matters to his millions of fans or lovers. He exudes the charisma of a typical Leo stud. He roars out his music, and at the ripe old age of fifty-nine he is still going strong. He still has sold-out tours and supermodel lovers after forty years in the business. His stage presence transcends time, and he will always be one of the great kings of rock and roll. This guy is luck on legs and he should inspire any of you Leos. Mick Jagger proves that, without a shadow of a doubt, Leos have more than their fair share of charisma.

King of rock and roll Mick Jagger

On the Other Hand . . .

Most Leos are very lucky. It's very difficult to find an unlucky one, because even well-known Leos who have suffered misfortune have also experienced amazing triumphs.

Amelia Earhart was a true adventurer. In the 1920s, she became one of the first female pilots. She also drove a bright yellow automobile (just like a Leo). Automobiles were rare in those days in general, and it was even more rare to see a woman driver. She loved speed and was determined to fly and test the boundaries of aviation. At that time planes were very risky and accidents were common. Amelia had several accidents when she was first training, but nothing would deter her passion for flying. She was the first woman to fly across the Atlantic.

Not satisfied with that great feat, Amelia wanted to be the first woman to fly around the world. She had decided that this would be her last challenge and then she would feel complete. She tragically disappeared without trace from that trip. Looking back, it seems that she may have sensed that this trip would be her last. As a Leo, play it safe: Don't push your own boundaries too far, and pay attention to your gut feelings.

Harness the Fire

Adventure is very important to you. If your life becomes too routine, you will end up like the big cats of Africa, lying around catnapping and waiting for your next big feed. Plan an adventure today: Decide to take that trip hiking in the mountains, or join that day-long class in race-car driving. Keeping yourself fit, active, and stimulated will not only increase your good fortune, but also your good mood. This is the first day of the rest of your life, Leo! Dance, sing, or do something unusual. Routine seriously drains your life force and you become a stir-crazy lion rather than the king of the jungle.

viRgo

August 23 – September 22

STAR pROFile

KEY WORDS	Responsible, meticulous, rigid, controlled
RULING PLANET	Mercury, god of communication
LUCKY AT	Accounting, analysis, law, commitment
AVOID	Judging, controlling, criticizing, celibacy

You Virgos have a bit of a reputation for being boring and always playing by the rules, although that is probably a vicious rumor started by a Sagittarian jealous of your ability to control your life. Of all the signs, you are the most likely to get rich and stay rich. You may not have as much reckless abandon as the other signs, and therefore slog your way to good fortune, but with a little fine tuning we can change all that.

You have an amazingly analytical mind and the most skill when interpreting numbers, and rumor has it you were put on Earth to be perfect and to serve. Now that sounds like a responsibility, and people presume it's your middle name! Mother Teresa was a Virgo, and is probably the only one who managed to live up to her own expectations in the servitude department. Even she probably still gave herself a hard time, and that's the Virgo dilemma.

You Have the Right to Be Wrong

News flash: There is no such thing as perfection! You are perfect exactly as you are, I promise! Lighten up while still paying attention to detail, and you can perhaps rake in those millions and still have a smile on your face. You sometimes feel as though you have to do something crazy and dangerous—not just to let your hair down, but also to prove to yourself and others that you are not as good as people think. Knock this behavior on its head by courting balance and stretching yourself to have fun without giving yourself a hard time at least once a week. Loosen up and you will be less likely to be self-destructive. Let's face it: That kind of drama-queen behavior is more suited to an Aries than you!

Of all the star signs you are the least likely to buy this book and the most likely to be drawn into more structured religious practices. If you are a contemporary Virgo, it is still tough for you to let yourself off the hook, and this can hold you back. You still catch yourself ironing your underwear. You may go out drinking and frolicking with your pals, have affairs, and take the occasional day off work with a hangover, but underneath it all you feel guilty. Guilt is one of the downsides to your sign. You can't or won't allow yourself to enjoy that day off because you feel bad. Get these

LUCKY GEMSTONES

Amethyst—a dark purple stone full of mystery and hidden knowledge—is your power stone. Hold it against your third eye when seeking solutions to complicated problems (but don't use amethyst if you suffer from paranoia or any mental illness). The Romans used to call amethyst "the sobriety stone," and it has been used to help people give up their addictions. The stunning **lapis lazuli**, that midnight-blue stone with gold flecks, was placed in the breastplates and crowns of ancient Egyptian high priests and was also sacred to the Babylonian goddess Ishtar, queen of the heavens and Earth. Place this regal stone beneath your pillow to open up your intuition and self-awareness.

clear-cut notions of right and wrong, good and evil, or black and white out of your head. Isn't it a bit extreme now that it's been pointed out? You are a mortal and as such are here to learn. If we lived in a perfect world where we all looked perfect and behaved exactly how we should, we would be Stepford wives and husbands and life would be very boring. Kick the guilt habit and you can use all those other marvelous qualities you have to better effect. What service does guilt provide anyway? It never stops you in the end, and if you have made a mistake you should love yourself through it rather than giving yourself a hard time.

You have been given just as much good fortune as the other star signs, yet allegedly your main desire in life is to serve. This is a bit of a chicken-and-egg dilemma. Do you serve others because you have to? Or do you think it is wonderful to be able to serve humanity? Start by serving yourself first. When you love and heal yourself, you pass that magic on. Don't leave yourself for last.

LUCKY *numbers*

Lucky numbers for Virgos are six, fourteen, twenty-three, and five. Six is a great number for you. It chills you out, connects you with your emotions, loosens you up, and gives you a sense of well-being. You are the sixth sign of the Zodiac and are ruled by the sixth house, and you therefore love this number. Six is the number of Venus as well, and although she is not your ruler, her energy is great to have around as it relates to love, harmony, and emotions.

LUCKY COlORS

Traditional colors like navy blue and hunter green resonate with you, as do indigo and deep purple (which reveal a deep inner wisdom). These colors relate to the third-eye *chakra*—the place of your intuition. Don't overdo them, or they will stifle your character and leave you too wrapped up in your inner world. You think about things intensely before you act, and these colors nurture and protect you. A small private room or study decorated in dark blue and green will give you peace of mind and encourage you to find answers within yourself. In this room, you can truly relax. You are not one for outrageous colors, such as fluorescent pink or lime green, but allow yourself to become more adventurous with your color schemes—particularly with your clothes—and you may find yourself with increased confidence. Allow yourself to explore. Add a bit of deep purple, to awaken your intuition and inner wisdom. When in doubt, you tend to go for the traditional look (unless you are in wild Virgo mode). Purple connects you to what is actually right for you! You have every right to be the unique being that you are and, with a little gentle nudge from Purple, you become more open to a rich inner world that was previously unavailable to you.

Verbal Virgo

You may be drawn to a career in numbers in some way, such as banking, accounting, or computer programming. As your ruler is Mercury, you also make an excellent communicator. This should give you a clue to the secret freedom you crave inside. Mercury is elusive and difficult to pin down, something you may secretly long to be. You are mercurial in your own way; you long to let yourself off the hook and when you learn to do this in a safe way you are a genius, full of incredible ideas, as well as a fantastic problem solver. When you brainstorm you can resolve anything. You are a great proofreader and can spot a mistake from a hundred yards, but you also have a hidden creative side and would be a great writer yourself. Don't view your creativity as nonsense—as a child of Mercury you have a unique voice and much to say. If you avoid being judgmental, you will find that your imagination runs very deep. I know a Virgo who secretly writes erotic fiction that would make the wildest Scorpio blush! Embrace your creative ability and it will enhance your life experience.

You might, however, want to make certain that you are very clear about expressing your wants and needs. Use your skill! You have many expectations about the way people should behave, and

Virgo Tip

You can have the tendency to feel overly responsible and get caught up in doing the "right" thing. Over time this drains you and makes you miserable. Schedule a day during which it is your duty to be frivolous. Go and spend some money on something decadent and playful. Buy a bottle of champagne or expensive, sexy underwear. Buy something you have always wanted but couldn't justify. Practice being a little less good—not your other extreme of being wild and out of control, but just a little naughty and unpredictable!

you want them to be telepathic when it comes to meeting your needs. You think that they should know how to act and what to do to make you happy. This has caused you all kinds of misery in the past, and you may have thought that you have bad luck with friends, lovers, or even family because you feel let down. The real truth is if you simply state what you need, and don't have a silent expectation just waiting to be broken, life will be a lot smoother. All successful relationships are about communicating and expressing your needs, and we all live in our own realities with differing ideas of how to behave and our own moral structure. Be clear about what your expectations are, and others will have the opportunity to please you. If you talk about your feelings without giving someone a guilt trip, you will find yourself surrounded by an abundance of love that is just waiting to be unleashed onto you!

Harness the Earth

Virgos can be very precise and pay an extraordinary amount of attention to detail. This is fabulous, and will aid you in any career you choose. You are fantastic at planning—from your garden to the interior of your home. But what about your spirit? Being an earth sign, you have a deep connection to nature. Follow this visualization exercise to feel grounded, safe, and balanced. Sit with your back against a large tree and visualize that your back is part of the trunk. Feel yourself grow roots that go far into the ground, taking nourishment right up through your body, filling and enhancing your spirit. Sit like this for several minutes and don't forget to thank the tree when you have finished.

Lucky Virgo

Sizzling Sean Connery, one of the sexiest men in the world, is a Virgo. Brought up in poverty in Scotland, he was the son of a truck driver and a cleaning lady. Sean dropped out of school at the age of thirteen and started delivering milk. He then went on to join the navy, but eventually received a medical discharge due to stomach ulcers (this can be a typical Virgo problem—all the worrying you do, caused by your tendency to want life to be just right, can cause stress-related illnesses if you're not careful). Sean tried his hand at professional soccer and even came third in a "Mr. Universe" contest before he found his true calling—acting.

Most people know him best as the ever-popular James Bond. Of course, not wanting to be typecast, Sean went on to make other films such as *The Untouchables* (for which he won an Oscar). In one poll he was voted the man that most women wanted to wake up to and have breakfast with, and he has never lost his good looks. Like most Virgos, he is known to be very opinionated, particularly about his native Scotland, which he adores.

Lucky Virgo Sean Connery taking a ☞
break during a game of golf

On the Other Hand . . .

River Phoenix tragically died at the age of twenty-three, at the peak of his career, of drug-induced heart failure. This brilliant young actor had always had a controversial life. His parents were members of the group Children of God, labeled by the press in the 1970s as "Hookers for Jesus." River spent much of his childhood there with his siblings Rain Joan of Arc Phoenix, Joaquin Raphael "Leaf" Phoenix, Summer Joy Phoenix, and Liberty Mariposa Phoenix—not the ideal environment for a Virgo.

He was an untrained actor who was a perfectionist and an observer of life. He always seemed to get the role just right. He made some profound films at a very young age, such as *The Mosquito Coast* with Harrison Ford and the highly acclaimed *Stand by Me*. He was nominated for an Academy Award for his role in *Running on Empty*. He died in his siblings' arms on the sidewalk outside the notorious Viper Room in Hollywood. The lesson to be learned from this for all Virgos is to avoid swinging to extremes.

Naughty Hugh Grant, although lucky in many areas, was famously caught in a compromising position with a hooker in Los Angeles just as his career was taking off. He had previously been known as the archetypal English gentleman. His lapse in judgment did not affect his career negatively at all, and in fact, may have helped it along.

But Virgos, beware: If you repress your sexual appetite or become judgmental and puritanical, your animal urges may overtake you so that you do something self-destructive or rash. Find the balance and accept your human side. Let your hair down more often to prevent the occasional, totally over-the-top wild time that could lead you into trouble.

1*i*bRA

September 23 – October 23

Star Profile

KEY WORDS	Balance, harmony, charm, friendliness
RULING PLANET	Venus, goddess of love
LUCKY AT	Relationships, diplomacy, the law, socializing
AVOID	Mood swings, moaning, pessimism, indecision

You have had many talents and gifts bestowed upon you by your ruler Venus. You give off a certain charm that is irresistible and have the ability to attract friends in droves.

Your missions in life are balance and thinking, which can lead to procrastination. Life for you is like walking a tightrope: You feel like you have to get everything just right in terms of balance. This task sometimes feels overwhelming and can seem to be a curse rather than a blessing, especially as you can have wild swings between what you see as good fortune and hard times.

Your scales sometimes tip from left to right in such a frenzy that you can feel seasick. The trick for you is to know that you are in charge of this internal rhythm. Unlike a fire sign, whose luck comes from action, or a water sign, whose luck comes through intuition, your luck (as an air sign) comes from inside you. What you think, you create.

Mirror, Mirror, on the Wall . . .

Because Venus likes to keep close tabs on you, you can get a little too interested in your looks. Librans tend to come from two camps: They are usually either overly concerned with their appearance, or look like they've been dragged through a hedge backward! This is another example of the swinging scale that influences all Librans, although it can give you the edge in areas such as fashion. You could make an excellent makeup artist, or even a storefront designer. You have a sense for what looks good and love to be surrounded by beauty.

You love the company of other people and would do very well as a party organizer or the owner of an art gallery. You have a keen eye and are stimulated by visual images. You have also been given the gift of excelling in relationships and have a mission in life to seek the perfect partner. As you are objective and have this skill, you would enjoy running a dating agency. In all of the above areas you will have exceptional talent, but you will excel at whatever you turn your hand to—as long as it feeds your soul. Deciding upon your profession probably took you an extremely long time, but once on your path, nothing can stop you.

Be Decisive!

This may sound simple, but for you making a decision can be a laborious task! You hem and haw over the tiniest issue. Even when making up your mind about something as simple as whether to have a glass of merlot or a vodka tonic, you weigh each choice like St. Michael weighing the souls of the damned, only to find when you have made the decision that you feel you probably made the wrong one. If you can relate to this, then you are aware that you can be overanalytical. Your special talent is for thought, so use it as a sword and cut away your fears. Write down what is bothering you, stick it in an envelope, and leave it alone: The answer will come to you without you even trying to find it.

Having the gift of thought as your good fortune is as wonderful as owning a Ferrari; it is such a powerful tool that you can be caught up just sitting in the driver's seat. The solution to your dilemma is not to overuse it. Just as you don't have to drive three hundred miles per hour because you own a Ferrari, don't overthink small problems. If you heed this advice it will release you from your occasional moodiness and sense of powerlessness. Less is more in your case, because you are the owner of a brilliant mind.

To increase your chances of success, aim for a career in which you have the space to excel at thinking. Librans make stunning lawyers and revel in anything legal, as justice is your forte.

Inside a Libra

So what about your emotional life? This, too, can be quite complicated. You tend to have periods when you are single, followed by long relationships that occasionally last longer than they should. Learning to let go when something is finished will energize your life. Trusting that love is destined for you as a child of Venus will make the in-between times fulfilling and filled with personal growth. Your ruler, Venus, is not only the goddess of love, but is also a great help in all matters to do with the heart.

If you have a love problem, why not perform a little ritual and ask for a resolution? Write a letter to Venus on a Friday (as that is her day). In Roman times it was perfectly normal to write a letter to the gods requesting that a wish be granted, and many people have had remarkable luck doing just that. Write a list of what you are asking for, make an offering (such as roses, Venus's favorite flower), and light a candle to send the prayer up to the gods. Take

LUCKY GEMSTONES

Jade has a cooling effect on your mind and is great if you are feeling mentally burned out or overloaded. Jade is purported to have five benefits: benevolence, integrity, wisdom, steadfastness, and courage. Many ancient cultures, particularly the Chinese, believed that jade was a sacred and lucky stone. The cheerful **sapphire** brightens you up and inspires you to express yourself, be creative, and have fun. Blue is related to the throat *chakra*, and this stone can help you express your emotions. **Green aventurine** and **opal** are also lucky for you.

advantage of your link to this benevolent ruler and give it a try. You have nothing to lose and everything to gain!

People are automatically drawn to your lovely nature and charm and you are a great mediator. As you get older (after the age of thirty) you build up a strong will like a rod of iron. No longer the pushover of your youth, it is perhaps then that you start to increase your wealth and sense of inner peace. If you are younger, practice being aware of where your personal boundaries are and say "no" when you mean no. Your caring nature can lead you to take a back-seat in terms of business, as you love to see others do well. Put yourself forward for that promotion or go after that audition—move toward your goal—success awaits you.

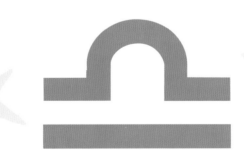

LUCKY *numbers*

Your lucky numbers are seven, sixteen, thirty-four, and six. Seven is the number of spirituality and contemplation. You are ruled by the seventh house and are the seventh sign in the zodiac. You have an air of spirituality and intensity about you, and because of your connection to Venus, you have a lot of extra charm. If you choose to live in a number seven home or notice that seven crops up frequently in your life, you are being urged to connect with your spiritual side. Meditate and take time out to contemplate without losing yourself in thought. The number seven allows you to get answers not from your rational mind, but from your inspired mind.

LUCKY COlORS

Pale pink and green are your colors. These relate to the heart *chakra*, the energy center of unconditional love. As Venus is your ruler, your heart center is usually quite clear. You feel deeply and have a strong desire for emotional balance. If you feel out of sorts emotionally, visualize a light pink or green color entering your heart area. Feel all your negative emotions dissolve as the pink or green restores your positive feelings and bathes you in unconditional love. Pink is an excellent choice for a bedroom because it is the color of love and allows you to open up to your emotions. Sometimes you have the bad habit of analyzing your emotions or feeling disconnected, but this color returns you back to you. Wearing pink also suits you and makes you feel more open to the outside world. If you're a man, you may have some resistance to wearing pink, so try to carry around a small card painted a vibrant pink and, if you are stressed out, take it out of your pocket and stare at it for five minutes. People may think you're a bit mad, but it really will work!

Lucky Libra

One could say that Michael Douglas was born lucky. As the son of Hollywood superstar Kirk Douglas, Michael was born with acting genes. He has always taken his career seriously and strove to be independent, achieving fame without his father's help (although he did work as assistant director for many of his father's films in the 1960s). He first became a big star in the TV series *The Streets of San Francisco*. Michael tried his hand at producing movies and won two Oscars for *One Flew Over the Cuckoo's Nest*. He seems to have the Midas touch. He went on to take up acting again and had huge hits with *Romancing the Stone* and *Fatal Attraction*, and was ranked as one of Hollywood's most powerful people.

He is now married to the gorgeous and much younger Welsh beauty, Catherine Zeta-Jones, with whom he has a baby son. This man could be said to be one of the luckiest men on the planet! His Libran eye tends to get the answer right every time.

Lucky and hugely successful Libran Michael Douglas ☞

On the Other Hand . . .

Montgomery Clift was one of the most handsome actors of his time. His Libran charm meant that he was pursued by Hollywood. Hesitant at first, he entered into a contract with one of the leading studios on his own terms (Librans are great at negotiation). He was a huge success and was nominated for an Oscar for his role in *From Here to Eternity*. He always seemed to have Libran mood swings, never finding the right balance between working and partying. Librans need space for peace and quiet, and if they are overworked they tend to get grumpy and unhappy.

Due to exhaustion, Montgomery had a car accident that injured his face. Although he had many friends who supported him and despite plastic surgery that nearly returned him to normal, he never seemed to recover his outgoing personality.

Balance is the key to happiness for Librans. If you find yourself disgruntled, look at which areas of your life you are neglecting. The most beautiful things about you are your spirit, energy, and charm. Never think it is all about your looks—you're a star just as you are.

Harness the Air

Your scales can become easily unbalanced, so it is essential that you make the most of your intellectual ability and focus your mind to avoid having a merry-go-round of ideas in your head. Write down any problem that is worrying you, and then write down all your worst fears about it. Take the papers outside and burn them in a fireproof dish, saying, "I release my fears to the universe to transform into a solution." Then, go back indoors and write down as many creative solutions to your problem as you can think of. Instead of focusing on an immediate change, think of small steps that you can take to improve your situation a little bit at a time. Taking life one day at a time will give you your power back.

scorpio

October 24 — November 22

StaR pRofile

KEY WORDS	Sensual, sexual, deep, intense
RULING PLANET	Pluto, god of the underworld
LUCKY AT	Seduction, investigating, researching, unearthing
AVOID	Manipulating, unfaithfulness, secrets, fear

Well, Scorpio? Are you lucky or not? You have no doubt had an interesting life, because that is your karma here on Earth—to go deeper. Being born a Scorpio often means facing a challenge in life, particularly in childhood. You have probably experienced more intense pain or disappointment than most, and some people may even say that to be born a Scorpio means that you lack good fortune. In fact, it was probably a Scorpio who said this.

There is a Chinese curse that says, "May you be born in interesting times," and your life is definitely interesting. You were also born oddly suspicious, perhaps with the underlying knowledge that you had your work cut out for you on this journey. Perk up:

It's not all bad. Far from it! The gods wouldn't leave you in the lurch like that. You were given unique gifts to help you on you way and to ensure that you succeed.

Savvy Scorpio

One of the major elements of good fortune bestowed on you is your intuitive ability. You have X-ray eyes when it comes to seeing into the souls of other people. You can tell if someone is lying to you and you instantly get to the heart of people. One scan with those sparkling Scorpio orbs and you sense all the fears and vulnerabilities hidden beneath the surface. This little trick has made you slightly paranoid that others can see your weaknesses, so you tend to hide beneath a façade that only makes others more determined to get to the bottom of you. Hide and seek is part of your nature—you run, and people chase. They back off, and you get concerned and turn on that Scorpio charm.

Your ruler is Pluto, lord of the underworld. Pluto, icy cold and dark, is the farthest planet from Earth. To have Pluto as your leader requires you to learn the cycle of life, death, and rebirth. Once you have overcome your fears you should have more knowledge and power than the rest of us mere mortals.

LUCKY GEMSTONES

Opal is considered to be a stone of doom by many, but this is actually your birthstone! The magic of opals is that they exaggerate whatever is going on with you, so you should therefore only wear one when you're feeling happy and energized. **Garnet** is a root *chakra* stone and balances and reawakens your sexual desire. If you have been feeling in a passion rut, carry this around with you to invoke steamy encounters. **Smoky quartz** is deep and dark, just like you. Use this crystal as a friend and ally to face your fears and release the past.

LUCKY COlORS

Your colors—dark red, black, and maroon—are all representative of the root *chakra*: the energy center around your genitals and center of the "fight or flight" impulse. A somewhat prehistoric center, this chakra and its colors relate to survival and embody, for example, the basic instinct to escape the saber-toothed tiger. They represent the mythological underworld of your unconscious. Death, sex, and rebirth stem from this area, and it is essential that it is balanced. You are drawn sometimes to a kind of Gothic melancholy where you see everything in black and white. When you slip into the underworld of your emotions you may suffer from pessimism and depression. Unlike other star signs, it is not wise for you to overindulge in your colors. Yes, sometimes it's great to crawl under your blood-red quilt and hide from the world, but come out occasionally to bathe in the lighter aspects of life. Lighten up your home, and, if you wear black all the time, mix in bolder colors such as yellow—the color of optimism.

Will You Crawl or Soar?

The scorpion is just one of your symbols; the other is the magnificent eagle. You have a choice in life: Which of these you want to be? Do you want to soar above the world, examining life from above, or crawl around, defensive and lowly? You have great gifts and potential, and it is important that you don't get caught up in the more sinister aspects of your personality. Your depth is a gift—your charisma and your understanding of life and death.

Here's more good news: There are thousands of famous Scorpios, because this sign knows how to succeed. Marie Curie, for example, used her depth to unearth the benefits of the dangerous element radium and changed the face of medicine. She was the first woman to win two Nobel Peace Prizes at a time when women weren't even allowed to lecture. You will succeed against all the odds; you are not only a survivor, you're a winner. You turn disaster into triumph, and when you learn to be optimistic, that's when the real miracles begin.

Your tendency to be obsessive can be turned into a positive quality as long as it doesn't overtake you in relationships. You will not give in until you have achieved your goal. This is a great quality, but sometimes you have to learn when to let go and move on.

You have a second ruler who gives you a dynamic edge, and that is Mars, the god of war. You won't let anyone get the better of you. If you let go of your strong temptation to seek revenge when hurt, you will be blessed with extra energy to put into other areas. Many comic actors—including Goldie Hawn, Danny DeVito, and Whoopi Goldberg—are Scorpios. Comedy is, after all, the flip side of tragedy. To be a great comic you have to understand the depths of life, and that is something you excel at. You are also totally irresistible and have the ability to capture the hearts of people for life. You make an excellent therapist as well, as you can see deep within the psyche of your fellow humans.

Bring It On!

Life may take you to hell and back, but you tend to rise up each time. In some cases you can have triple the luck of other people because you have such a strong antenna for the undercurrents that occur in life. You may be very good with the stock market or with building up an industry that is need-based. You love to succeed, and to have that desire takes you halfway to your goal. Optimism is the key to turning your life around. Believe in yourself and the fact that life wants to give—not take—and you will exude much less energy worrying and more time reveling and enjoying life.

You are the world's best lovers. This is not a legend—it's true—and you know it because you have a special touch that takes your partner to join you in the underworld of life. You will unearth all your partner's secrets but not necessarily reveal much about your own (well, maybe in a few years). You are truly loved and adored by people who sense that you don't trust easily and feel honored that you have chosen them. If you believe in reincarnation (and you probably do), then this life is probably one of your most important. Because of this, you will have chosen to master your own trust issues so that you can open up to all that is around you.

Scorpio Tip

Remember the first law of gravity:
What goes up must come down. Add this to the wisdom from the wheel
of life: What goes down must always go up. Remember that life is a
cycle and you are going to experience all of it. If you catch
yourself feeling miserable and uninspired, know that life
can turn around from one minute to the next. Live
in the present and enjoy every minute of it,
because you may win the lottery; you
might get a parking ticket and fall in
love with the officer serving it; you may
buy a picture of an emu at a flea market
and discover it's a Picasso! Treasure and
joy are always on the verge of finding you.

Lucky Scorpio

Whoopi Goldberg was not born lucky. Her amazing wit and
Scorpio charm led her to the top the hard way. Her earlier careers
included being a bricklayer and a funeral makeup artist. She
dropped out of school, took drugs, and then married her drug
counselor. When the marriage split, Whoopi took off and originally
changed her name from Caryn E. Johnson to Whoopi Cushion. Her
mother allegedly said that she wanted her daughter to be more
respectable, so she changed it to Whoopi Goldberg. Like any
evolved Scorpio she is a natural at comedy, and her inspired one-
woman show won a Grammy Award. From there she progressed to
acting and was nominated for an Oscar for her role in *The Color
Purple*. She won an Oscar for her hilarious performance in the film
Ghost. It wasn't luck that got Whoopi where she rightly deserves to
be today, but rather pure Scorpio grit and exceptional talent. You
often have to make your own luck if you are a Scorpio, but like
Whoopi, no matter how far down you go, you can rise even higher.
She went on to host the Oscars in 2002 and stole the show.

Lucky lady Whoopi Goldberg ☛

On the Other Hand . . .

Sylvia Plath was consumed by the Scorpio shadows of death and depression. A talented and intense woman, she penned such profound works as *The Bell Jar*. Scorpios often experience situations that involve death and rebirth, either symbolically or literally. You need to understand that death is just another passing phase into a different experience, not an ending. Scorpios seem to fall into two camps: those who have no fear of death and those who are obsessed with their own and others' mortality.

Sylvia's father died when she was eight and it left a deep mark on her. She suffered from depression from an early age and attempted suicide many times. Her creativity seemed to save her occasionally, but she suffered from an inferiority complex and felt she would never make it. This was perhaps intensified when she married the famous poet Ted Hughes. Unfortunately, after a tempestuous relationship Ted had an affair and Sylvia eventually killed herself. This dark tale sends a sharp message for you Scorpios to make peace with yourself. Do not give in to self-doubt and fear. Your ability to travel to the depths of life graces you with wisdom, depth, and the ability to rise like the eagle and soar. Trust in life and you will be pleasantly rewarded.

LUCKY numbers

Scorpio, your lucky numbers are eight, thirteen, nine, and three. Thirteen is unlucky for some, but your mystical edge makes this number strangely useful for you. The digits in thirteen add up to four, which is a number of security and balance. Oddly, thirteen may make you feel safe, as you probably love the mystery that the number thirteen connotes. If you are drawn to it, use it as a talisman and no doubt you will be able to transform the power of this number into something profoundly positive.

Harness the Water

Land scorpions can't swim and don't like water, and even water scorpions are reluctant to swim! In many ways it's bizarre that you are a water sign at all! Here are some tips to survive your element. Water symbolizes the emotional flow in your life. If you feel that your life is a stagnant pond rather than a tropical water garden, sort out the backlog of feelings. Go to an anger release class and scream or take up kickboxing to release that pent-up energy. Even better, take up writing poetry. Find an activity that will release your emotional energy and soon you will be free from the murky swamp of the past and swimming with the dolphins.

Scorpio Tip

You are naturally psychic but tend to see the negative rather than the positive. Practice developing your intuition by creating a meditation space where you can go and focus purely on positive insights. Keep a diary of all the good things you would like in your life and all the positivism that you experience daily. If you catch yourself thinking a negative thought, turn it around. If you meditate for just ten minutes every day, you will notice that your life becomes more productive, lifting your spirits and introducing you to the great possibilities for joy in your life. The universe loves you and wants the best for you.

SAGITTARIUS

November 23 – December 22

STAR PROFILE

KEY WORDS	Free spirit, upfront, honest, eccentric
RULING PLANET	Jupiter, god of good fortune
LUCKY AT	Travel, adventure, philosophy, exploration
AVOID	Being unpredictable, changeable, defensive, insecurity

You Sagittarians have been surrounded by good fortune, with a special talent for optimism. You have the heart of an adventurer and the desire to quest forth in life to discover what it's all about. This perception of the world as a playground is not in the least superficial: You really want to experience being alive and also to understand why you are here.

You cannot fail to have some good fortune in life, as you are already blessed by your ruler, Jupiter—the planet of good fortune. Jupiter will always help you no matter how dire your circumstances. Something always saves you at the last minute. You might be hanging off the side of a cliff, clinging on by the tips of your fingers, when a trained monkey (freshly escaped from the circus) throws you a rope attached to a tow truck and you are hauled to safety. The monkey's owner—who is stunningly gorgeous—turns up and immediately asks you out on a date. This story could happen only to you!

Salacious Sagittarius

Sagittarians are eccentric in an attractive way. You are bold and forthright, always speaking your mind. You sometimes put your foot in your mouth, but you are loved for this and easily forgiven. You hate to be bored and try to stay active. This leads you to more good fortune. You're an excellent dancer and a great traveler. Foreign environments appeal to you more than any other star sign, and you are often planning your next expedition in your head. The joy of traveling for you is twofold: Travel always changes your life path and, nine times out of ten, it's for the good, and you meet interesting people who can help you or have a message for you. If you haven't been aware of this, pay attention on your next trip.

You are a philosopher, filled with a natural depth of knowledge. You will never conform just for the sake of it—you always go your own way. For you, personal freedom is everything. You can't stand people who are small-minded and judgmental, because you believe everyone has the right to journey through life with free will.

It may take you a while to find a mate who can fit into your self-constructed world, but when you find them they tend to stay. You will not commit yourself before you are ready, and often have passionate short-term relationships before finding your soul mate.

Sagittarius Tip

Watch that mouth of yours! You
tell it like it is, and while this is one of your most endearing features
(and, in a sense, should make everyone around you feel safe) it can
screw up your chances of succeeding. If you tell your boss that
he's an idiot for not signing that business deal, you
might be right. However, he will not want to see
your face around the office. The delightful
thing about you is that this actually
surprises you! Ideally you should
work for yourself, but remember to
check that tongue of yours! Jupiter
will always bring good fortune
your way—lucky you!

LUCKY COLORS

Your colors are bright pink, electric blue, violet, and bronze. You are drawn to colors that make a statement. Even if you are a more conservative Sagittarius, you will no doubt have some bold color statement in your home. Your colors are connected to the heart, the throat, and the third-eye *chakra*. This means that you have a passion for freedom of speech and are very intuitive, with an innate curiosity for all things philosophical. You love being alive, and your effervescent personality enjoys splashes of color and all things different. This is fantastic, but perhaps it would be wise for you to have a

plan before you begin. You tend
to purchase different objects like a
magpie, grabbing whatever takes your
fancy. Work out a way to bring these
different styles together. Perhaps invest
in some small, tester paint cans before
leaping into some brash new color
scheme for your home. You are so
inventive and spontaneous
that you may end up with decorating
disasters if you aren't careful.
Planning is essential; otherwise
your home may become a
strange mixture of differing
styles and ideas that even *you*
can't appreciate!

Sensually Skilled

You have great stamina as a lover and an extremely amorous nature. Impulsive and adventurous, you know how to satisfy your lover, and are among the top four lovers of all star signs, along with Scorpio (although they can be a bit manipulative as lovers and use sex as a weapon), Aries (who have your stamina but lack your foreplay skills), and Pisces (who have the romance and gentleness but not your vigor).

Your only fault is that you don't like to be pinned down. You have the spirit of an adventurer and you can't put up with people you consider to be foolish. This can land you in shark-infested waters, because while you blow your stack and then forgive, others do not forget your harsh words so quickly. Your overall sexiness, however, helps you: You have an animal magnetism that makes others want to please you. That can't be bad, can it?

Any job in the travel industry will bring you success. You'd also make a great teacher or lecturer because you have a passion for learning. This enthusiasm is contagious. You are a stunning athlete, and apart from recklessness you excel at all things physical.

Kahlil Gibran, the author of *The Prophet,* was a Sagittarian who put his philosophical bent down on paper. He wrote one of the most profound books ever written, but arguably never repeated this brilliance. Sagittarian inspiration is not something that can be captured: It has a mind of its own. If you are inspired, do something with it now. Never wait!

One of the few sketchy things about your personality is that you are quick to anger and can appear irrational. You have a very set view of your own personality and have created a mini-universe in your mind where there appear to be a whole lot of rules that go against the status quo. As you haven't written a manifesto and tacked it on your bedroom wall, lovers and colleagues may encounter these rules unawares. If they make the fatal mistake of breaking one of your unique and elusive rules, you explode—much to the incredulity of the person involved (who may only have stirred their coffee in the wrong way). However, you don't mean any harm and are totally without malice—just passionate about life. This quickness to anger needs to be explained and admitted to for you to free yourself and be the wild soul you are. Learn to think before you fly off the handle.

Lucky Sagittarius

Aristotle Onassis, John Paul Getty, and Conrad Hilton were all eccentric but wealthy Sagittarians. J. Paul Getty was said to be worth about $4 billion when he passed on at the age of eighty-three. At one time he was thought to be the richest private individual in the world. Some people thought he was moody, because he continually bemoaned the fact that people were after his money and expected him to tip well, and he once made comments about how a billion dollars wasn't what it used to be! He certainly must have had some luck to achieve such a vast amount of wealth. Funnily enough, his alleged moaning and cheapness is a very un-Sagittarian quality, as you are typically very generous. Getty felt that his penny-pinching mentality was the only way to become a millionaire, so perhaps this is wise advice for you. He even had a pay phone in his mansion so that his guests wouldn't feel that they were imposing by using the phone!

Wealthy Sagittarian John Paul Getty ☛

On the Other Hand . . .

Bruce Lee, possibly the most famous martial artist in the world, was a typical Sagittarian. His physical prowess and swift-moving style were no doubt helped by his star sign. He fought discrimination and prejudice in Hollywood for years and finally achieved success with *Fist of Fury*. It is rumored that Bruce was supposed to play the lead role in the television series *Kung Fu*, but Hollywood racism prevented this. In true Sagittarian style, this further spurred Bruce on to succeed. Just as his star had finally risen he suffered a brain edema and died. Bruce's film, made for $500,000, has since gone on to gross $1.2 million.

LUCKY *numbers*

Lucky numbers for Sagittarians are nine, eighteen, thirty-four, and three. The number nine gives you the courage and strength to be the person you were born to be. If you live in a home with a nine in the address, or are drawn to this number, it will allow adventure and passion to flow freely and will transform you into the god or goddess you are! Nine bestows on you your own natural vibration, and when you're around this number, things tend to go smoothly. Three is a great number if you want to lay foundations or build something from scratch.

Harness the Fire

You are an entrepreneur and have lots of ideas of what you want to do in life. Life for you has to be an adventure, and no matter how boring or mundane your life is now, you—perhaps more than any other sign—can succeed in exploring the world. Never forget that travel is what you are here to do. A rare few of you may not like physical travel, but will be fascinated by armchair traveling, studying philosophy, or metaphysics. You thrive on learning. Whichever of these pursuits turns you on, it is essential for you to follow through. Get up now and go take a class or open up a map and decide which country you want to journey to.

Sagittarius Tip

Travel not only inspires you, it has
the capacity to turn your life around. When you travel you find your
power, facilitating the beginning of a new cycle for you. If you're
stuck in a rut, emotionally drained, or heartbroken, plan a
trip. If you ask the universe to bring you the answers to
your problem, they will appear as if by magic on
your journey. You'll meet people who will
help you (though you won't know it)
and unusual coincidences will occur
that will guide you. When you return
home, your thoughts will be clear and
positive, and your life-affirming
energy will be renewed.

CAPRICORN

December 23 – January 20

STaR pROfile

KEY WORDS	Responsibility, disciplined, hardworking, riches
RULING PLANET	Saturn, god of hard lessons
LUCKY AT	Making money, business, banking, building
AVOID	Rigidity, being judgmental, control, sternness, aggression

Of all the star signs you are blessed with the ability to achieve your goals. It will take hard work, but you have the capability to be very wealthy indeed. No matter what circumstances you were born into, you can climb to the top of the tree. Many Capricorns start with nothing and climb to meteoric heights. Like the goat, you tenaciously climb until you reach the top, happily chewing on grass along the way if need be, before you find your oasis in life. You are guaranteed success if you persevere. Other signs get bored before they make a million bucks, but achievement is in your blood.

A Driven Spirit

Once you achieve what you have worked for, God himself couldn't pry it from your clenched fingers. If you are that rare creature—the unsuccessful Capricorn—get focused! There is no doubt that you can rise beyond your dreams.

You are ruled by Saturn, the planet of tough learning, but you are not afraid of hard work and most of your lessons are learned in your childhood. You are a master of self-discipline and this is one of the parts of your nature that helps you achieve your purpose.

Others perceive you as stubborn, pigheaded, and downright difficult, but actually you are just single-minded. You have a very strong sense of responsibility and will work as hard as ten men if must. You are very committed to your work and wonder why everyone else can't live up to your standards. You never disrespect your boss but always have your eye on their job. Being too serious at times makes others trust you but remain cautious friends. Open up a bit more. Most important, make time for play!

You can be a bit of a control freak, particularly as a boss. You know exactly what you want and need from colleagues. You do get frustrated and impatient, but you are the epitome of a professional.

Capricorn Tip

Rule (if you must) with an iron fist in a velvet glove.
You have a tendency to railroad people if you think you are right, and
could be accused of having impossibly high standards. We are all
different and each have our own unique view of how much
is enough and what constitutes perfection! Even if
you're right, you might try persuading people
with charm rather than commands.
Charm will help achieve your goals
and retain the goodwill of your
colleagues. Good fortune is based on
a little bit of karma: What ye
sow, so shall ye reap!

LUCKY COlORS

Capricorns have some dull colors associated with them: brown, charcoal, and gray. Consider picking colors outside of this conservative range. You look fabulous in all shades of brown, black, and charcoal, but what the hell do you wear in the summer? White is an excellent shade for you. Orange is great to get you going, as it spins the wheels of your sacral *chakra* (the energy center around your navel). This is the center of creativity and sexuality and will boost your energy levels. Yellow will also cheer you up. If you're prone to weight gain, don't paint your kitchen orange, or you will eat more! Maybe it is time for you to let your hair down in the decorating department, and become more sprightly with your sense of fashion. Buy a few modern style magazines and peruse them at your leisure. No one is asking you to rush in or do anything rash, but check out the latest looks and find one that suits you. Think of some colors that you like but were afraid to try, and if in doubt ask for help (yes, I know you find that tough but it could bring you closer to your partner or friends if you share this intimate change with them). You will love having the latest trendy look, as long as it's classy too—just like you!

Never Give Up, Never Give In

Professor Stephen Hawking, a well-known and tenacious Capricorn, overcame many odds to achieve worldwide success with his book *A Brief History of Time*. It broke a number of sales records and reached the number one spot on many sales lists in three days. Although he was at the time suffering from a progressive neurological disease (Lou Gehrig's disease), he did not let anything get in the way of having a full life. One of the Capricorn gifts that Stephen clearly has is that he never felt sorry for himself and rose to any challenge. The most famous Capricorn of all, of course, was Elvis Presley. He rose from a dirt-poor family to be staggeringly successful and rich. Martin Luther King Jr. was also a Capricorn. King made a huge impact on the world by fighting for justice and equality. He died for his convictions, and that is the length you will go to if you believe in something strongly enough. You have some great role models—more than any other star sign. You can rise from nothing to the top, and the astonishing thing is that if you really make your mind up to do something, it will happen.

You are also alarmingly quick-witted and can use this to delight or destroy. You know what weaknesses others have and sometimes play cat and mouse with them. You have a temper when annoyed,

Lucky Gemstones

Diamonds (of course it had to be something expensive!) inspire you, give you bright ideas, and even lighten you up. They make you feel content and self-assured. **Tiger-eye** stimulates your intellect, cocoons you with protection, and gives you added insight into yourself. **Moss agate** reconnects you with nature and your roots. You will feel grounded and connected to your environment if you carry this stone. It may inspire you to start gardening or get outside more often. That's not a bad thing, is it?

but it does not usually explode (like a Sagittarius). You will toy with your prey before destroying him completely.

You live in your head and often find it challenging to discuss your emotions. You hate to be vulnerable and see these discussions as weak. Overcome this and you will have more allies. People think you are indestructible and this is not at all true; in some ways you need more support than anyone (if only you would admit it).

Learn a lesson from Howard Hughes: He achieved total financial security, but, apparently, never personal happiness. At the end of the day you need to find balance. Lady Luck is with you all the way, and you don't have to make a choice between relationships or success. This all-or-nothing stubborn attitude blocks your path. Try not to be so hard on yourself and those close to you. Underneath that tough exterior you're a teddy bear who craves affection and deserves to be adored and cherished. You are as solid as a rock, but be sure to let the love in and allow others to take care of you and give you lots of attention.

Loosen up! Life is so much more pleasurable when you let yourself go a bit. Instead of believing that you have to work eighteen hours a day, seven days a week to succeed, change your thought pattern to one of receiving all you desire easily and smoothly. It will happen; keep heading up that mountain.

LUCKY *numbers*

Lucky numbers for Capricorns are ten, eight, one, and eleven. Eight resonates to Saturn—your ruler—and gives you an austere sense of safety. If you are wealthy and have achieved a lot of what you desire, then this number is great for you. Living in a number eight home when you already have good fortune can help you keep it for up to twenty-eight years. If, however, you are unlucky or lonely, avoid a number eight home like the plague because those qualities could also stay with you for twenty-eight years! One is a great number if you are starting new projects and want the energy and drive to succeed.

Lucky Capricorn

Mel Gibson was born in the United States before he emigrated to Australia with his family at the age of twelve. He breezed into acting and his first major film was the cult classic *Mad Max*, for which he was paid only $10,000. Mel went from hit to hit, and finally won two Oscars (Best Actor and Best Director) for *Braveheart*. Unlike almost any other big Hollywood star, Mel has been happily married for twenty-two years and has seven children. He has never been linked to a love scandal and adores being a regular family man. He always makes sure he has enough time for his family during his busy filming schedules. As if this wasn't enough, he seems to grow more gorgeous each year and is still considered one of the sexiest men in Hollywood. His regular-guy attitude and charm make him one of the nicest as well as the luckiest men in the world. If you want it, Capricorn, learn Mel's lesson: Balance family (and your social life) with business.

Lucky Capricorn actor Mel Gibson ☞

On the Other Hand . . .

Janis Joplin was one of the biggest singing stars of her time, yet has been forgotten by many people under the age of thirty. She had an amazing voice and a rock-and-roll lifestyle to rival any of the male rock stars of the time. She was a sex, drugs, and rock and roll goddess who did it her way. Unfortunately, her way killed her at the tender age of twenty-seven.

No matter how successful she became, a part of her suffered horrendous insecurity. During high school she was nominated (probably by some jealous Virgo prude) for the dubious award of "ugliest man." Despite all the taunts, she climbed to the top of the tree, as any decent Capricorn would. She was worshiped by millions for her uniqueness and her transcendent sexiness that, though not conventional, was a Capricorn earthiness much like Elvis's. This genius died a rock-and-roll death because she did not believe in herself, and there is no place in a Capricorn heart for self-doubt. You're fantastic—live it!

Harness the Earth

You know enough about work to write a dozen books on how to succeed. Even if you hate your job or loathe your boss, you work hard and have all the ability required to succeed. Harnessing the earth is not your problem—letting go is! If you have kids, take them out and do something frivolous. Jump on a trampoline, go ice-skating, or build a tent in the backyard. If you don't have kids, borrow some! Your friends will be pleased to get a babysitter and you will learn the joy of play. Get in touch with your inner child. Go skate-boarding or get into a water fight with the garden hose: Anything to lighten up! Children often have more to teach us than adults do, for children teach spontaneity.

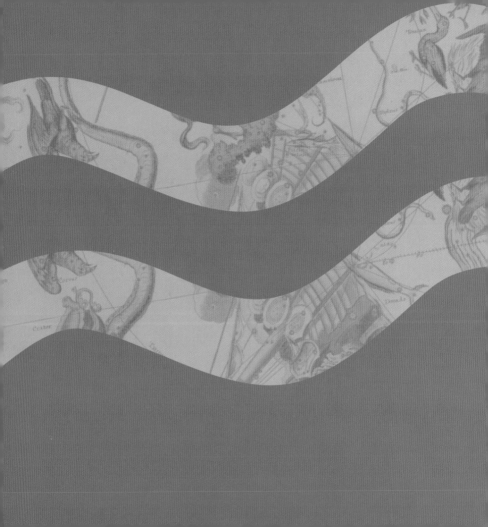

AQUARIUS

January 21 – February 19

STAR Profile

KEY WORDS	Humanitarian, freedom, equality, androgyny
RULING PLANET	Uranus, god of individuality
LUCKY AT	Inventions, speculation, trends, originality
AVOID	Detachment, overanalyzing, kinkiness, aloofness

Well, Aquarius . . . not only are you packed to the gills with an abundance of fine gifts from the gods, but as we are also living in the age of Aquarius you have an opportunity to shine if you so desire. You are a visionary in a time of visionaries, and the only thing that can stop you is if you leave all those wondrous ideas in your head rather than bringing them into concrete reality.

You are a fantastic creature who not only has ideas ahead of your time but also has a fierce compassion for others. You see personal freedom as being a divine right and you are always aware that we are all equal, regardless of race, sexuality, disability, or politics. Ruled by Uranus, you are automatically infused with a desire to be a free spirit and hate any kind of restriction. You may feel that you have a certain androgynous quality, and you don't like to be defined in terms of your gender.

Acute Aquarius

You have a keen, scientific mind and are normally ten or twenty years ahead of your time. You know what social values we will all have in the future, and you are drawn to computers and all new forms of communication. Don't take this kind of knowledge for granted: If you tap into it you can make a fortune. You are a brilliant inventor and can develop huge ideas from just a tiny seed. There are more geniuses in your star sign than probably any other. You have that genius gene as part of your heritage from the eccentric Uranus. Many Aquarians are inventors or discoverers, including Galileo Galilei, the famous astronomer and inventor. Fascination with time and space can be a preoccupation of yours, and there can be almost an otherworldliness about you.

As the water-bearer, you also have a fascination with science fiction and UFOs. It will probably be an Aquarian who first makes contact with extraterrestrials. You have a gift not only for astronomy but also for astrology and space travel. You have an interesting ability to intellectualize about sex like Alex Comfort, who wrote *The Joy of Sex*, and Virginia Johnson, the sex researcher. You make excellent writers, too. Is there anything you're not good at?

Aquarius Tip

Stick to one thing at a time and practice the
art of completion. You have so much energy that you rush from idea to
idea without ever finishing the job properly. If you could pace
yourself and take on a little less, you would get much better
results. You often wonder why nothing finishes well for
you, but if you monitor your commitment to
each project (including your love life)
you'll know why. If you put all that
ingenuity and imagination into one
area, it would blossom. You hate to be
pinned down and work in quick bursts,
leaving you drained and tired. You have
genius in your bones, so use it wisely!

LUCKY COLORS

Aquarians look stunning in silver, bright blue, and turquoise. Blue is the color of the throat *chakra*, a place where you speak the truth. Unlike most other signs (except Aries and Sagittarius) you have no problem speaking the truth or expressing your thoughts. What you feel is perhaps another matter, but you live to communicate. Talking, sharing ideas, and solving problems are your strong points. Choose pink to encourage your emotions, or orange to light your creative abilities and unleash a more earthy sexuality! Use silver for protection and as a magical shield to fend off pessimism. Imagine a silver light cocooning your body: This will protect you and keep you uplifted, particularly if you are around less enthusiastic people. Sometimes you are like an excited bubble, and less inspired mortals seem to want to prick that bubble with a needle of discontent. You often bound into a room full of vision and excitement and get discouraged by the negativity of others. If you can seal your aura with a silver light, then nothing can hold you back.

Quirky and Eccentric

With all this exceptional brilliance you can't help but shine. Some people, however, don't seem to get you. Maybe it's your liberal attitude or your funky clothing, but you always stand out in a crowd. You will not conform to the norm and always need to express who you are. Others can get wound up and emotional in an argument, but you are strangely detached: You use your brainpower rather than your emotions to win debates. Fortunately, this does not usually bother you. You don't care at all about the opinions of others and have a natural self-esteem that carries you through life relatively unscathed.

You hate injustice and do not like anyone gossiping about you, but you will see that as an error in them rather than anything to do with you. You will fight for what you believe in and seek a higher purpose in life. If you're not careful you can get too caught up in drugs or excessive partying. If you were born at the right time you probably were tempted to try these or their opposite, evangelical religion. Anything that takes you to other realms tempts you, as sometimes you may even think you were not destined for this planet at all and were dropped off in the wrong place. This is because sometimes you still have your head in the clouds.

LUCKY GEMSTONES

Turquoise has the dual effect of inspiring and grounding
you so that you will be able to bring your visions to life. This
stone has a visionary quality. Find a piece with silver flecks to really
light your fire. This stone is completely at home with you and you should
notice immediate benefits when you wear or carry it. **Amazonite** infuses
you with a sense of adventure and the need to explore new frontiers
either mentally (by taking up a new area of study) or physically
(by tracking through the mountains of Peru, for example).
This is a particularly good stone for women.
Hematite is a stone that boosts your self-esteem
and sense of self. If you are feeling down or
not quite yourself, this shiny silver
stone is for you. If you have to
give a talk or perform on
stage, hematite also
guards against
stage fright.

Exercising that monumental mind of yours will give you inner peace, but make sure you find a balance. If you're feeling headachy or spaced out, take time out to do something grounding like jogging, ice-skating, or gardening—anything that is connected to Earth through which you can channel good energy.

With an Aquarian, what you see is usually what you get and you don't understand manipulation or underhanded games. You allow others to be themselves and become confused if they aren't as straightforward.

Great magic awaits you, and all you have to do is tap into it by allowing your brilliance to turn into concrete reality. You may have a strong yearning to form a band, go to drama school, travel to the Serengeti to find an herb that will end disease, or escape to a monastery in the Himalayas to contemplate the meaning of life. Whatever you want to do, try it. It's only when you try it that you will know if it is what will bring you inner peace. You have so many adventures in your head that the danger is that you won't do any of them. Whether you know it or not, you are an inspiration to others. It may take years for people to appreciate the message you are spreading now, but it will get there in the end.

LUCKY *numbers*

Lucky numbers for Aquarians are eleven, four, twenty-two, and forty-four. You are especially drawn to the two master numbers—eleven and twenty-two. Like you, these numbers have a special magic and energy in them like no other number on earth. These numbers will lead you to your inspiration. It may be a tough journey, but you will get exactly what you deserve in life with these numbers behind you. The more you put in and the more you are true to yourself, the greater the rewards!

Lucky Aquarius

What a woman! Not only is Oprah Winfrey one of the richest women in America, she is also one of the most loved and revered. Hers is a real rags-to-riches story. She survived and triumphed over her past to create a talk show that was ahead of its time. Her show also works to fight social injustice and attempts to enlighten and heal America and the world. It has a fresh brand of honesty, depth, and integrity. What an achievement! A true inspiration to all of us, this astounding Aquarian has single-handedly shown all people in the universe how to succeed, follow their own path, and live a life full of purpose. She is a beacon of hope and lets us believe that we, too, can achieve our souls' potential and find our calling.

Lucky Aquarian Oprah Winfrey follows her own path ☛

On the Other Hand . . .

Rasputin, in typical Aquarian fashion, was ahead of his time. He was alleged to have sensed the future and held sway over all of Russia. A letter he wrote to the Empress Alexandra did appear to predict certain events in Russian history, including the death of the empress and her family, who died nineteen months later. Rasputin was also said to have healing powers that helped a member of the royal family with hemophilia. To this day, doctors are baffled as to how he managed to achieve that.

This religious man also drank like a fish and had a voracious sexual appetite. Like most Aquarians, he didn't care what others thought, and ended up being murdered by irate relatives of the Russian royal family, who thought his influence would bring about the end of Russia. The lesson to be learned by you Aquarians is this: Avoid the vodka and don't go out carousing! But seriously, don't get carried away with your vision.

Harness the Air

You are **wildly inventive**, which can come through in lots of different ways. You may come up with gadgets that make life easier, like an alarm clock that doubles as a fruit smoothie maker. Or **you may be talented at mixing music** and coming up with **unusual beats or styles that are really original**. You **might just be great in the sack**, and carry out unknown sexual miracles for your lover. Whatever way your inventiveness manifests itself, **turn it to your advantage and don't take it for granted**. Nurture and encourage whatever inspires you, for **you have multiple talents that you don't use** that could make you a **small fortune**!

pisces

February 20 – March 20

STAR PROFile

KEY WORDS	Romantic, creative, compassionate, spiritual
RULING PLANET	Neptune, god of the sea
LUCKY AT	Drama, healing, creativity, poetry
AVOID	Daydreaming, lying, fantasizing, fickleness

Darling Pisces, how gentle you are. You were placed on this planet with open heart and an imagination that stretches from one corner of the Earth to the other. Your gift is your sensitivity, although sometimes you would gladly sling this back in the face of the fates! You have a profoundly romantic and creative streak and a gentleness that resonates with intuition. You may feel that the world is too harsh a place for you; when you agreed to be born (you have a strong belief in reincarnation and all things mystical), you were expecting beauty and tranquillity—not the mayhem that we call home. In fact, it's as if you dropped from heaven itself and your mission is to bring a little bit of that love and faith with you.

Pisces Tip

You respond so well
to nature. Make sure you take enough
trips to parks or to the countryside, particularly if you live in a city.
Being alone is an essential part of your nature that is often denied,
because your deep love and nurturing spirit make you a
magnet for anyone with a problem. Remember: You
are not a charity and you have to take time out
for yourself. Give yourself some love and
nurturing, and make sure you have a
sufficient support network for
yourself. You have an excellent sense of
the flow of life. When you tune in and
make space for yourself, life just
automatically goes in the right direction.

You have the ability to write the most amazing poetry or draw pictures that capture the essence of what you are sketching. If you don't feel you have these gifts it is probably because you are naturally a bit insecure and don't always believe in yourself. Give it a whirl: Sit down and try to draw or write and you will be pleasantly surprised. Inspiration will soon come. Don't give up on the first attempt, but keep at it. Expressing your emotions is essential to your mental and emotional well-being.

Sensitive Fish

You hate loud people and big noises, although you do admire and gravitate toward confident and successful people. You do not see success as a materialistic endeavor—it's about finding out what your soul was put here to achieve and achieving it. Unevolved Pisceans may be tempted to live in a fantasy world, even by lying. They can lose themselves in the Neptunian depths of alcohol or drugs, or maybe even sex addiction. The good news is that you Pisceans can't ignore your inner voice that tells you to stop.

Many Pisceans set the world to rights by writing or creating (for example, books, movies, etc.). This naturally creative ability, which can capture the hearts and emotions of others, is an essential element in our society; without your emotional input and intuitive love we would all be living in darker times.

Your intuition is one of your main strengths. If you develop it, it will always help you out of trouble. You have a direct line to the heavens and the answers will always appear to you if you are listening. When you practice listening to your gut instincts—and are not swayed by the honeyed words of a charmer—your life will profoundly shift to one of total serenity. Don't let paranoia be mistaken for intuition. You can tell when you are being paranoid because it will come from a place of fear and insecurity rather than from that wise sage within.

Many Pisceans become interested in their own spiritual development and make excellent psychics. Profound wisdom comes easily to you. Meditation is also particularly good for you, but be careful that you don't waft away on a diet of spiritual excess that can be just as dangerous as any other extreme.

You sometimes mistakenly think that love and romance are the keys to your happiness. So many Pisceans have had to learn the lesson that the more they seek love, the less they find it. If you love yourself and life, true love will leap out from behind a corner one day and surprise you with all that you desire. Go hunting for it and it will be more elusive than the last unicorn.

LUCKY Gemstones

Amethyst helps prevent your addictive nature, and is great to meditate with if you feel you are going a little over the top on the alcohol front. **Pearls** are from the sea and allow you to connect with your emotions. They may make you a little weepy, so only wear them when you want to release your emotions. **Aquamarine** is a gorgeous stone. In its raw state it resembles a chunk of the ocean. An instant calmer, this gem soothes you and washes away any fear or negativity that may be lurking in your sensitive spirit. Place this stone under your pillow for a peaceful night's dreams and to encourage a chat with your spirit guides who will give you dreams rich with answers.

Fabulous You!

Your other fabulous feature is your generosity of spirit and thoughtfulness. Other, more cynical signs, like Capricorn, may think you're crazy to be so giving, but you sense that what you give will return to you tenfold. Anyway, what would life be like if there was no giving? You love to give presents and cards to people to show you care. Because you have this element of unconditional love, you apparently have a bigger guardian angel than the rest of us. Someone definitely looks over your shoulder, and when times get really tough and you are really down, a little voice tells you that it will be okay, that dreams really do come true, that love is just around the corner, and that soul mates do exist. This keeps you going and your dreams do come true in the end—usually even bigger and better than you could have possibly imagined.

You are an ideas person and have great vision. Perhaps you need to develop your practical skills to make your visions reality, but you have the power to succeed because your vision of business always touches people's hearts. You may develop a face moisturizer with a crystal at the bottom of the container that becomes visible when empty, or diapers with fairy tales printed on them. Whatever you develop, it will no doubt bring comfort and nurture. Try not to lose yourself in fantasies or daydreams, but work each day toward making your dream life a concrete reality.

You have so much to give, but often feel like you need to withdraw because of your sensitivity. If you embrace the great spiritual truth that nothing is personal, and that all of us are doing our very best in the moment, you will feel much better. We all create our own different realities here on Earth and have our own interpretation of life. No two people ever experience the same thing, even when in the same room together: Try asking two people to recount the same event and you will be astounded by the different stories they tell. You of all the signs get closer to a real union with people. Just be aware that they have their own reality.

LUCKY COLORS

Your colors—lilac, sea green, mauve, and aquamarine— are related to spirituality, the misty shades of the waters of Avalon and the Lady of the Lake. You love the King Arthur myth as it embodies so many different meanings, notably magic, romance, and loyalty. These colors soothe and calm you, bringing you balance and inner clarity. Aquamarine is connected to the throat *chakra*, and is great to meditate upon as it helps you to think clearly and to express your emotions. Visualize a sky blue light entering your throat, releasing negativity and allowing you to express your inner truth. Wear a blue scarf or carry a piece of aquamarine around with you to help you communicate your needs. Sometimes you get so caught up in your empathy for others that you neglect your own needs, leaving you feeling hurt and resentful. Remember, it is your responsibility to ask for what you want. You were born to express yourself and with your creativity you can do anything——you have a special magic inside waiting to get out.

Lucky Pisces

Drew Barrymore started out lucky! She floundered later on with a brief love affair with drugs, but then rose to even greater stardom. Her first major claim to fame was at the age of seven in the blockbuster hit *ET*.

Life is always tough for a child star, and things were no different for our Drew. Although she has major acting genes—her mother, father, grandfather, and grandmother were all actors—Drew temporarily got off track when she allegedly started using drugs and alcohol at the age of nine, leading to cocaine abuse by age thirteen. By fifteen, however, she was drug-free and had taken control of her own life. She still had a bit of the wild child in her, but went on to reclaim her rightful crown as a leading actor in such popular films as *Scream* and *Charlie's Angels*.

Piscean angel Drew Barrymore ☞

On the Other Hand . . .

Elizabeth Taylor is the queen of Pisceans. Not only does she have the Sun in Pisces, but also fiery Mars, the planet of passion and vitality. Being one of the most beautiful and most highly paid women in the world did not stop Ms. Taylor's apparent misfortune. She has suffered terrible health problems, and fought an addiction to painkillers after a childhood riding accident that took place while filming *National Velvet*.

Elizabeth Taylor had a tempestuous marriage to the world-famous actor, Richard Burton, and seemingly succumbed to breaking the golden rule of Pisceans: Never drink to excess. Another husband, Mike Todd, died in a plane crash, and several other marriages failed. Coupled with her constant back pain and ill health, Elizabeth has had a rough ride. However, she is also a goddess of romance and has attempted to live all her dreams. That's what every Pisces should do!

lUCKY *numbeRS*

Pisceans' lucky numbers are twelve, seven, thirteen, three, and twenty-two. Seven is a particularly good number for you because it is the number of spirituality. It reveals mysteries and encourages trust. If you live in a home with seven as the address, lots of fated encounters with wise people will occur, and you will feel as contented within this place. If you have over-whelming problems, they will soon transform into opportunities because the number seven is about learning and growing. Twenty-two is a master number and those who are drawn to it have a mission to complete. Twenty-two guides you toward finding your higher purpose.

Harness the Water

Y ou are possibly the only true water sign because you live totally in the water and couldn't survive outside it. You are a creature of the lakes and sea, which makes it difficult for you to survive the harsh realities of the practical world. Your symbol depicts two fish swimming in two different directions, so you often swim in circles in your everyday life or feel as if you are being pulled in two different directions. Learn to communicate with both sides of yourself and come to a unanimous decision, rather than changing your mind, then changing it back again. This behavior not only drives you nuts, but everyone around you too. Use your intuition and make decisions you can stick to.

Pisces Tip

You are the most creative sign and when you express your artistic side, good, productive energy starts to flow. Allow yourself to try out all the different creative techniques that you like, even if you don't think you're any good. Drawing, painting (even if it's just finger painting), music, and writing all help you affirm your life force. Don't get lost in depressing poems or songwriting but allow yourself to write a celebration of life, expressing the diversity of your emotions. Go to drama class because that's where you can boost your confidence socially, too. Get creative— you will be astounded by the results!

Dedication
To Marie: Always be safe in the knowledge that wherever you swim, a large ram with plastic flippers and a snorkel will never be far behind! E.L.

About the Author
Michele Knight (*www.micheleknight.com*) is a wild Aries woman who has been a psychic since birth. Her mother is a well-known Italian psychic and medium. Michele has been a media psychic for many years and regularly appears on television and is astrologer for a magazine. Michele has been practicing intuitive astrology since the age of thirteen and lives with her Piscean soul mate, sixteen cats, and two dogs in a secluded country cottage.

Picture Credits